To:

Enjoy

Allan Waddy
23/5/2024

Guilty

Knowledge

Canadian True-crime Cases

Allan W. Waddy, CD
Private Investigator

Guilty Knowledge

Copyright 2020 © Allan W. Waddy

All rights reserved.

The author may be reached at:
aceinvsec@shaw.ca

ISBN: 978-1-7751763-0-5

Guilty Knowledge

Canadian True-Crime Cases

Allan W. Waddy, CD
Private Investigator

**SHORT STORIES PUBLISHED
BY ALLAN W. WADDY, CD
Available for viewing at**
www.allanwaddy.com

Driving Into Danger
Reeled In
Dad's Dieppe
The Horrors of Dieppe & Beyond
Snow Storm
Cornwallis
UNDOF
Maggie & the River

**TRUE-LIFE ADVENTURE
BIOGRAPHY**

Buckshot & Johnnycakes
(2019 Best Sellers List)

Dedication

To my amazing wife & business partner,
Gloria Rose Waddy:

The Truth Shall Set You Free
John 8:32

.

TABLE OF CONTENTS

1	Introduction – Definitions & Canadian Legal System - Criminal Case #1 – Murder of Leading Seaman Gerald Mulholland	1
2	A New Career	21
3	Civil Investigation Case #1	35
4	Surveillance Case #1	46
5	Criminal Case #2	54
6	Surveillance Case #2	62
7	Criminal Case #3 - Suicide by Police	70
8	Child Protection Case #1	78
9	Criminal Case #4	89
10	Intro to Fire & Explosion Investigations	97
11	Fire Investigation #1	109
12	Fire Investigation #2	124

13	Natural Gas Explosion Case #1	129
14	Accelerant Fire Case #1	138
15	Fire Investigation #3	145
16	Civil Investigation Case #2	150
17	Civil Investigation Case #3 - The Cover -up Murder of Johnny Sticks	160
18	Criminal Case #5	166
19	Surveillance Case #3	179
20	Criminal Case #6 – The "Wonky Eye"	187
21	Surveillance Case #4	200
22	Surveillance Case #5	205
23	Domestic Civil Case #1	211
24	Civil Investigation Case #4 – Project L.U.C.I.D.	218
25	Surveillance Case #6	231
26	Surveillance Case #7	237
27	Surveillance Case #8 – The Watch Cow	243

28	Surveillance Case #9 – The Rambling Handyman	248
29	Fire Investigation #4	251
30	Fire Investigation #5	258
31	Suspicious Death Case #1 – The Florida Scam	269
32	File Intake Preparation	282
33	Bar Surveillance #1 – The Eye is Quicker than the Hand	288
34	Surveillance Case #10	293
35	Surveillance Case #11	299
36	Civil Investigation Case #5	306
37	Fire Investigation #6	318
38	Fire Investigation #7	323
39	Fire Investigation #8 – The Hot Wire	328
40	Taking down the Shingle	336

FOREWORD

This *True-crime* vignette is a distillation of thousands of civil, criminal and surveillance files successfully concluded by my wife, Gloria and I. These true-life stories incorporate a selection of investigative files conducted on Vancouver Island, mainland British Columbia and the United States; during our twenty-six years of operating Ace Investigations Inc.

     The names of all parties have been changed and/or omitted to respect the privacy of the innocent and in consideration of the guilty that have paid their debt to society; although it is legal to disclose the names of convicted persons, as criminal hearings and sentences are public knowledge. The unbalanced scales depicted on the front cover of this non-fiction book were significantly balanced as a result of the successful conclusion of the random cases encapsulated in *Guilty Knowledge.*

Allan W. Waddy, CD

CHAPTER 1

Introduction – Definitions & Canadian Legal System
Criminal Case #1 – Murder of Leading Seaman Gerald Mulholland

Guilty knowledge is a term that refers to having knowledge that "*a wrongful act or situation exists, but a person chooses to ignore, or commit a crime, violation, or a wrong, especially against moral or penal law.*" A trained (Private) investigator is able to recognize guilty knowledge in the course of investigating crimes or offences. Success of any investigation is a culmination of experience, the use of investigative tools and, the ability to look at the evidence without bias: *as contempt prior to investigation is abhorrent*.

Some of the basic principles of Canadian criminal law are, of course, *Presumption of Innocence*, *Due Process*, *Independent Judiciary*, *Openness, Accessibility of Court* and, *Equality Before the Law* - just to name a few.

It was not until April 1982 that Canada amended the *British North American Act* (BNA) through enacting amendments to the *Canadian Constitution*; effectively becoming law known as the Canadian *Charter of Rights and Freedoms* which also guaranteed rights of Aboriginal peoples of Canada; provided for future constitutional conferences and set out the procedure for amending the constitution in the future. The new Charter had a far reaching impact on law enforcement as, for the first time in Canadian history, the constitution protected citizens' rights in the process of investigation, consideration of arrest and affecting the laying of a charge: regarding search, seizure and right to legal counsel. The new charter literally changed law enforcement and gave a whole new meaning to the term *guilty knowledge*.

The British North American Act was written and forged into law by the fathers of confederation in 1867 and, in 1873 Canada's first Prime Minister John A. Macdonald, formed the North West Mounted Police (NWMP); affectionately referred to as the Mounties, thereby bringing Canadian authority (to the then) North West Territories which is now Alberta and Saskatchewan.

NWMP jurisdiction grew to include the Yukon in 1895, the Arctic Coast in 1903, British Columbia and northern Manitoba in 1904. In the same year, the name changed to the Royal Northwest Mounted Police (RNWMP) and, in 1920 the RNWMP absorbed the Dominion

Police Force and became the Royal Canadian Mounted Police. The Mounties were frontier policemen and well known for their scarlet tunics.

In 1858 the British Columbia Provincial Police Force came into effect and proudly policed the province of British Columbia until August 15th, 1950. The BC Police Force came under the jurisdiction of the RCMP "E" Division which took over policing of the province for the second time in 1950.

Today there are only three Provincial Police Forces in Canada: Ontario Provincial Police (OPP), Quebec Provincial Police (QPP or Surète du Quebec) and the Royal Newfoundland Constabulary (RNC). (*Wikipedia*).

In addition, the Canadian Forces Military Police (CFMP) are classified as Peace Officers within the Criminal Code of Canada through an Act of Parliament, and provide policing, security and operational support to the Canadian Armed Forces and the Department of National Defence worldwide. The CFMP routinely functions within the civilian, criminal and military justice systems, and are classified as peace officers within the criminal code; which gives them the same powers as civilian law enforcement personnel in their ability to enforce Acts of Parliament on or in relation to the Department of National

Defence (DND) property or assets anywhere in the world. (Military Bases, United Nations (UN), North Atlantic Treaty Organization (NATO) mandates or, Military Attaché).

Canadian Forces Military Police have the powers to arrest anyone who is subject to the Code of Service Discipline, regardless of position or rank under the *National Defence Act* (NDA). CFMP have the power to arrest and charge non-Code of Service Discipline bound civilians only in cases where a crime is committed on or in relation to DND property, assets, or at the request of the Minister of Public Safety, Commissioner of the Correctional Service of Canada or the Commissioner of the Royal Canadian Mounted Police. During the October crises of 1970, Parliament gave the Canadian Forces authority to patrol the streets of Quebec and the city of Ottawa. This was invoked by former Prime Minister Pierre Elliot Trudeau under the *War Measures Act*.

Prior to the unification of the Canadian Forces on October 1st 1968, the Royal Canadian Army (RCA) was policed by the Canadian Provost Corps (C Pro C), the Royal Canadian Airforce (RCAF) was policed by the Air Force Police (AFP) and, the Royal Canadian Navy was policed by the Shore Patrol (SP) under the jurisdiction of the Judge Advocate General (JAG), Legal Branch of the Military. In the case of the Royal Canadian Navy, where I learned my trade, the administration of justice (discipline) on a Canadian Forces naval ship is commanded by the Commanding Officer with delegated powers to the Executive Officer (Second in Command) to affect discipline on the ship's company; with additional authority given to the Coxswain - the senior chief petty officer onboard the Ship. Officers were disciplined by higher authority.

The Queen's Regulations & Orders (QR&O's) are amplified by Canadian Forces Administrative Orders (CFAO's) and Naval General Orders (NGO's) were the legal directives in administering discipline, punishment and committal as necessary. (NGO's preceded CFAO's).

My primary function on the ship was Captain's Secretary, responsible to the Commanding Officer for the preparation and maintenance of all personnel records, legal documents: charge reports, conduct sheets and committal orders under the authority of the Commanding Officers Powers of Punishment Table (*National Defence Act*).

A trial at sea is referred to as the *Captain's Table* and the Coxswain is the senior non-commissioned officer responsible for administering discipline to NCOs and crew members under the direction of the Executive Officer. Discipline matters onboard commissioned warships are dealt with by summary trials and court martials: both administered for punishable offences under the *National Defence Act* (NDA). Both the Coxswain and Captain's Secretary work out of the Ship's Office; with one side of the office being the Captain's Secretary's desk and the other side being the Coxswain's desk (Regulating Office).

The commanding officer (minimum naval rank of commander on a warship or the army rank of lieutenant-colonel) has the authority to administer punishment to all ratings below the rank of Petty Officer First Class (Warrant Officer): usually heard by the executive officer and stood over to the captain. However; if the accused is a Petty Officer First Class (Warrant Officer, promoted by the House of Commons) and above, the commanding officer is required to *Stand Over* the proceedings to be heard by a squadron commander, who holds the rank of Naval Captain (army equivalent of full colonel). Generally, a court martial of an officer would be dealt with by the Assistant Judge Advocates Office ashore. In that exception, any member of the ships company charged with an indictable offence and, depending on the charge under the Code of Service Discipline, has the option to elect trial by court martial. During my time, we humorously referred to those charges as "hanging offences."

An example could be dereliction of duty, drunkenness on duty or a serious criminal offence (striking a superior officer); whereby the Powers of Punishment warrant imprisonment of two years less a day in a military detention barracks. The legal system onboard ship is a fascinating structure as even in a foreign port, unless the crime is committed against the laws of the visiting country, the ships company will be dealt with by the military authority of the naval ship.

As a point of interest, I was involved in a situation in a foreign country where a Canadian sailor committed an illegal act (robbery and assault on a foreign citizen) and the military member was charged, convicted and sentenced to imprisonment in the foreign country. That particular case occurred in Japan, and the member of the ship's company was tried by Japanese court, found guilty and sentenced to five years imprisonment with hard labour: to be served in Japan, in spite of the Canadian Navy's attempts to financially negotiate the convicted Canadian sailor's freedom. Unfortunately, the convicted sailor was released from the military and served the full five years in a foreign correctional facility; a prison that brutally administered hard labour: as the offence was a *crime of violence* under Japanese law.

In Naval shore establishments, discipline is the authority of the base commander and maintained through the shore patrol under the direction of the Master-at-Arms (senior chief) who is the regulating authority on the Naval base (shore establishment).

A poignant example of the military and civilian justice system cooperating was the case in the murder of Leading Seaman Gerald Mulholland, a father of seven children who was murdered while working part-time as a taxi cab driver in 1970, while stationed at CFB Esquimalt, the Naval base in Victoria, British Columbia.

Two young sailors and a civilian: Able Seaman Gary Smith (age 18), Able Seaman William Larlham (age 20), and a civilian Terrence Parsons (age 19), were drinking in the Churchill Hotel on Government Street, downtown Victoria on the evening of November 10th, 1970 and, around 7:00 p.m. the three men got into a C & C Taxi and left the Churchill Bar. Unfortunately, the part-time cab driver was Leading Seaman Gerald Mulholland, a Royal Canadian Navy sailor also serving at the Naval base at CFB Esquimalt.

Witnesses reported seeing the three men leave the bar and, after Mulholland picked the three men up it appeared that they were driven somewhere in James Bay, a suburb of Victoria, near the waterfront off Dallas Road. What the evidence pointed to was that the three fares robbed Gerald Mulholland and, that during the robbery, a sharp object pressed against

Mulholland's neck was determined to be the cause of death. The three men fled the area and on the late evening of November 10th, the victim was tragically found dead at the wheel of his taxi.

On November 12th, the Victoria Police Commission offered a $2,000.00 reward for information leading to the arrest of the perpetrators. Soon afterward, police arrested the three men and they were incarcerated and charged with murder. It was determined during the first appearance trial, presided over by The Honourable Judge William Osler, Crown Prosecutor J.W. Anderson, and Military Defence Lawyer Brian Smith that the two sailors would be tried in a civilian court.

As there were nearly 50 witnesses for the prosecution, the three-week trial was scheduled in the Provincial Court. Justice Osler stopped proceedings on day four of the trial and committed the three to a higher court; as the military base did not want to try the other two by court martial as a result of the third accused: Parsons, being a civilian; who later ended up being a witness to the proceedings.

During the trial, which was convened at the Victoria Court House on Burdett Street, in Victoria, it was determined that both sailors had been AWOL (Absent Without Leave) from the Military base at the time of the murder. Evidence at trial established that one of the sailors sitting in the back seat had placed a sharp object to the neck of Gerald Mulholland while trying to rob him and, in a sudden movement of the driver's head, the ice pick severed an artery in Mulholland's neck and he bled to death.

Both the accused Smith and Larlham were found guilty of non-capital murder and sentenced to fifteen years imprisonment; of which the first two years less a day was to be served at 14 Service Detention Barracks at RCAF Station Namao, then part of Griesbach Barracks and now Canadian Forces Base Edmonton.

During the court proceedings, I was attach-posted to the Admiral's Building at Maritime Forces Pacific Command Headquarters (MARPAC) in Her Majesty's Canadian Dockyard (HMC) Esquimalt and assigned as an administrative participant in the trial.

The murder of Gerald Mulholland was not only devastating to his family but deeply felt by the entire Pacific Fleet. Leading Seaman Gerald King Mulholland is at rest in Hatley Memorial Gardens Cemetery at Colwood, B.C. (across from the former Royal Roads Military College (RRMC). "LEST WE FORGET."

The British North American Act permitted an amending formula and changes were required through an Act of Parliament: whereas 50% of the populations in 7 of 10 provinces had to agree with the proposed changes. Quebec did not agree with the amending of the original Act, which was deemed by some constitutional scholars to be *ultra vires* (not legally enacted by parliament) and, in addition, Quebec stated that they did not need to agree with the amending formula because of the *Distinct Society Clause.* The entire process then became a source of considerable complexity.

For example, the failed Meech Lake and Charlottetown Accords, attempted to enact the *Distinct Society Clause* that to this day has evolved into a complex and, at times questionable interpretation of the original intent of the *British North American Act.* However, Quebec has never formally approved of the enactment of the amendment - though the Supreme Court concluded that Quebec's formal consent was not necessary.

Years after ratification, the government of Quebec passed a resolution authorizing an amendment. Some historians, politicians, law makers and legal scholars virtually shake their heads at the complexity of the *Charter*, as it is generally referred to in the Criminal Justice System.

The *War Measures Act* of August 22nd, 1914 was legislated by Parliament for the purpose of Canada declaring war at the onset of the First World War hostilities. However, as briefly touched on above, in October 1970, the Prime Minister invoked the only peacetime use of the *War Measures Act* as a result of the FLQ (Front de liberation du Quebec); the separatist kidnapping of Quebec Provincial Deputy Premier Pierre LaPort and British Diplomat James Cross.

The *War Measures Act* invoking of October 1970 has not been repealed and is still in effect to this day, although in 2015 the Canadian Parliament enacted the *Anti-Terrorism Act* (Canadian Government House of Commons Bill C-36 and 37-1) as a result of the 9/11 terrorist attacks in the United States. As a point of interest, I was stationed at *HMCS Hochelaga*, in Ville La Salle, a suburb of Montreal, in 1966 when the FLQ were threatening the security of military bases in and around the city of Montreal. During that situation, Canadian Forces personnel were required to patrol the perimeter of military bases in Montreal as a deterrent to insurrection.

The antithesis of that *Act* would be the example of the *Canadian Charter of Rights and Freedoms* harbouring and protecting Migrant Security refugees in 1999, at a time when the migrant boats plagued countries along the Pacific Rim, including Canada.

In early 1999, human smuggling of Chinese Nationals from the Fujian Province in China began as a human trafficking business that resulted in thousands of impoverished Chinese citizens being extorted in exchange for a new life in Canada, which the migrants were led to believe was the Promised Land. Organizers of the human trafficking schemes were named *snakeheads* (human trafficking leaders) because their organization was so deep underground that the only way to stop the trafficking was to "cut the head off the snake," thereby eliminating the source of the smuggling hierarchy.

The despicable *snakeheads* perpetrated the smuggling, migration and extortion of monies from Chinese families desiring a better lifestyle for their loved ones, resulting in theft of personal property, bondage, debt and, in many cases, death.

The smuggling ring, led by the *snakeheads*, went into impoverished Chinese villages and told the families that they would, for an exorbitant fee up front, and small monthly payments which could be paid later until the debt was liquidated: transport their sons and daughters; some women pregnant or with small children, out of the villages and move them by ship, tanker, freighter or whatever ocean going vessel was available; in consideration of a large cash fee. It was said that the fees were as high as $50,000.00 US dollars. The criminal organization convinced the elders that their fortunate sons, daughters and children would be taken to Canada, the United States or Australia and provided jobs and a place to live so that the chosen ones could send money back home to their families in China, thereby paying back the cost of the migration.

The migrant dilemma caused significant immigration problems for Canada; as at that time in history, Canada was the only country in the free world that, through the changes to our Constitution in 1982, protected and harboured refugees: whether by smuggling or declaring refugee status, especially when they entered our territorial waters allowing the migrants protection under the Canadian Constitution, assuring the refugees the right of protection, respect, dignity and free legal counsel - complete with an expedited hearing before the Canadian Immigration Department.

The first two Chinese tankers drifted into our territorial waters in the spring of 1999 and ended up in Port Alberni, British Columbia. The ruse, perpetrated by the migrant smugglers was to load hundreds of Chinese migrants into filthy and overcrowded vessels of various length and mechanical disrepair.

The vessels, commanded by sea farers hired by the *snakeheads,* would arrange for the dilapidated ships, usually 100 to 150-foot-long fishing boats or other small cargo vessels, to become disabled near or on the international territorial boundary along our coast line.

Near or inside our territorial waters, the vessels would send out an *emergency distress signal,* while drifting further into our coastal waters.

Receiving the Emergency Distress Call, the Canadian Coast Guard, Canadian Navy or independent high seas salvage companies would respond to the distress call, evaluate the situation and, if required escort the disabled vessels to the nearest port.

Upon boarding the filthy, stinking, human trafficking ships and opening the cargo holds, the shock of seeing hundreds of starving and half dead migrants crammed into the small cargo space, covered in human feces and wailing and crying from weeks of thirst, starvation and sea sickness, was beyond human comprehension.

The Royal Canadian Mounted Police, in consort with the Royal Canadian Navy, immediately became responsible for the well-being and placement of the suffering migrants.

After receiving medical attention, food and clothing, the migrants were transported to the military gymnasium at Work Point Barracks in Esquimalt, B.C. for internment until they could separate the migrants from the smugglers. It was human suffering at its worst and I profoundly applaud the Police Officers and Military Personnel who initially became responsible for the care, protection and custody of the refugees.

Under the aegis of the *Canadian Constitution*, the refugees were entitled to free legal counsel and, within days of being interned on the military base, a host of lawyers came forward as legal representatives for the incarcerated migrants.

Immigration Canada and our federal courts were overwhelmed and, as required by law, the migrants were released on the condition that they would return at a certain date for an *immigration hearing*. Unfortunately, of the 167 migrants who were set free (1999) through the Courts, only 28 were located and eventually brought before an immigration hearing.

The migrants that were able to land ashore and take up residence without being processed through immigration; were taken to sweat shops all over the Americas and the extortion began, whereas the smugglers confiscated the majority of their wages from placement in laundry shops, brothels or prostitution. Their families in China never heard from their loved ones again and, no money was sent home.

In June of 2000, Immigration Canada contracted with the Canadian Corps of Commissionaires (CCC) to provide Migrant Security Training overseen by the Royal Canadian Mounted Police; in anticipation of more migrant ships drifting into our territorial waters.

It was at that time, I was recruited, as a former law enforcement officer and a licenced security guard, to work and train with the CCC and the RCMP through the Western Communities RCMP Detachment. In addition to our crew, there were four serving RCMP Officers on the refresher course and, on completion of the training our team readied the gymnasium at Work Point Barracks for the anticipated arrival of future migrant ships.

The experience working with the migrant security operations was very valuable as we were trained in Chinese customs and re-certified in use of force techniques relative to guarding and protecting migrant refugees who would be destined for internment and processing through Immigration Canada and, eventually the courts.

Our team of migrant security officers was comprised of Commissionaires, serving RCMP Officers, serving law enforcement personnel from Victoria City Police, Saanich Police, Oak Bay Police and former law enforcement officers who worked and trained together on a *Standby Status* for approximately 11 months. Part of the training was detection of *guilty knowledge* in the manner in which the migrants communicated with the *snakehead* smugglers while in their physical presence. For example, out of fear of reprisals, the Chinese migrants would overtly avoid eye contract with the smugglers, thereby sending a message to their protectors as to who the smugglers were. The smugglers, attempting to avoid detection, would turn their faces and avert their eyes from the vigilant guards.

Fortunately, in the year 2000, the migrant ships moved further down the west coast and became the problem of Mexico, South America and eventually, Australia. Canada's interdiction was successful in eradicating human smuggling into Canada and, through the efforts of the Canadian Coast Guard and Canadian Navy patrolling the west coast; the migrant ships were deterred from entering our territorial waters. This was a joint effort working with the United States Coast Guard and United States Navy.

There are several investigative tools used by professional investigators to determine if suspects are exhibiting guilt, have knowledge of guilt or, expressly, have knowledge of a criminal act or the commission of an offense.

In civil law the legal system relies on the principle of: *"a balance of probabilities"* established and documented by case law. In criminal law, investigators are called to a higher standard of due diligence requiring a: "*preponderance of evidence*" and conversely being overseen by "*reasonable doubt*" and "*show cause.*"

This concept encapsulates the term *Reasonable and Probable Grounds* (RPG) where law enforcers require a much higher standard before arresting, restraining, searching, seizing and charging persons who may have committed an illegal act.

Guilty knowledge is not sufficient within itself to charge a suspect, as in the case of polygraph testing whereby those results are only considered an investigative tool rather than a means of establishing or, conversely, proving guilt.

In fact, a defence lawyer would most likely advise his client not to take a polygraph test based on the principles of the Charter namely: the "*presumption of innocence* and *self-incrimination.*" Also, the polygraph test is not admissible in a Canadian court of law.

A criminal charge of arson requires and demands a higher standard of proof establishing: motive, opportunity and a direct physical link to the scene and is a good example whereby the insurer (insurance provider) has the option to hire an independent or private investigator to establish or prove the claimant is guilty of arson and thereby *attempt* to deny insurance coverage.

Proof of arson alone is insufficient evidence to deny an insurance claim, or conversely, prosecute if there is insufficient evidence to charge the claimant. Of course, the law is clear in that a person is not permitted to financially benefit from a crime; wherein the burden of proof becomes even more stringent. Arson is an *indictable offence* and if there is injury or death as a result of that criminal act, the charge would most likely be *criminal negligence causing injury or death;* resulting in a conviction and imprisonment of anywhere from 10 to 14 years in a federal institution.

CHAPTER 2

A New Career

In the summer of 1990, after 27 years of service in the Federal and Provincial Governments, I struck out on my own. I was forty-three years of age at that time and had been working since the age of 15. The drastic adjustment to civilian life left me in a quandary, as I had been gainfully employed since my first job in a saw mill in 1962, highlighted in my biography, *Buckshot & Johnnycakes*.

At that time, my wife Gloria was employed as a Community Development Worker with the Valley Native Friendship Centre and I unexpectedly found myself sitting at home wondering what was next. On the day that changed my life forever, my wife asked me the question of the ages:

"What is the one thing that you always wanted to do?"

Without hesitation, I replied, "Private Investigations."

"Well," replied my brilliant wife, "make it happen."

Hearing those words, I Immediately

commenced compiling a list of all the transfer skills that I had acquired from the military, corrections work, law enforcement and general life skills and applied for a grandfathered private investigator's licence. On November 27th 1990, I obtained my Investigators & Security Company Licence from Security Programs, Ministry of Solicitor General, Public Safety Branch and opened Ace Investigations. It was an exciting new chapter in our lives.

Between November 27th 1990 and December 31st 2016, my wife and I investigated over three thousand criminal, civil and surveillance files for the Justice Department, law firms, insurance companies and a few private individuals. It was exciting work and I am thrilled to be able to share some of those files and experiences.

For the first three years after starting Ace Investigations, I learned new skills, took courses related to the Security Industry: Principles & Practices of Insurance, Fraud Examination Courses, Veritas (Latin for truth) Interview and Interrogation Technique Courses, Privacy Legislation Training and Fire & Explosion Causation Certification. In addition, I joined the Insurance Bureau of British Columbia, Canadian Association of Fire Investigators (CAFI) and International Association of Arson Investigators (I.A.A.I) and also became a certified member of the Council of International

Investigators: the elite world organization of Investigators. A few years later I started contract work through the *B.C. Justice Department*, an incredible opportunity for a self-employed private investigator. Through long hours, determination and good fortune, we were able to develop clients, purchase company equipment and get Ace up and running.

The days were long and difficult; however, in the spring of 1993, having secured a comfortable client base of contracts: insurance company clients, Workers Compensation Board, Insurance Corporation of British Columbia, law firms and a few private clients, I realized that there was more work than I could handle and asked my wife if she would consider leaving her career and commencing an apprenticeship in my firm.

Within three weeks of resigning her position; a brave move on the part of my very talented and well-respected wife, we started the next phase of a long and prosperous working relationship within the security industry.

The first order of importance was completing and submitting the paperwork to get my wife licenced as an *Investigator Under-Supervision* while creating a training plan whereby she would qualify, within four years, as an Unrestricted Licensee. In that regard, I designed a training plan using a model taught to me on Instructional Technique (SIT) Courses taken in the military, which, I understand set a new standard in security programs for future apprenticed investigators. It was exciting to develop and create a means whereby Gloria, and later, my daughter Dawn were able to acquire certification without having to attend expensive and time consuming training courses; courses which would be of little value, as very few security companies are willing to hire an untrained investigator since it is not financially feasible to have two investigators on one case.

The unfortunate part of an *Under-Supervision* Investigators Licence; although we fully agree with those regulations, is that a restricted licence means that the apprentice is not permitted to work alone and must be supervised by a fully licenced investigator. However; my wife was a quick learner and Gloria made a career decision early in her training that she wanted to specialize in *surveillance* techniques.

This did not present a curriculum development barrier as I had been trained in surveillance and observation investigations during my military career and eagerly began Gloria's training in all aspects of investigations, including surveillance.

Years before in 1979 while attached to the United Nations Observer Force (UNDOF) in the Golan Heights in Syria, Israel and (UNEF) in Egypt as a Military Observer, some of our duties entailed watching and recording peace treaty violations in the Middle East under the aegis of the Security Council Peace Initiatives - within the regions we were deployed.

Having my wife working in our company was most enjoyable and rewarding, contrary to the general consensus that married couples usually find it quite stressful working in the same office; however, by year three of training, Gloria had excelled as a surveillance investigator. She was a natural and having prior experience working with cameras and darkroom capabilities soon became an invaluable asset to law firms and insurance clients. After Gloria obtained her unrestricted licence, she was added as a Director in our partnership, Ace Investigations.

In fact, after Gloria was certified and came off supervision, we continued working as a team, when physically possible and, the new clients, hearing about our team would phone the office and enquire about the "husband and wife team of investigators." It was endearing and we complimented each other with our respective skills.

Our client base grew exponentially and, in 1995 we incorporated our growing security business and while I worked surveillance, civil cases and criminal files, Gloria became fully immersed in surveillance operations. By this time, we were working all over British Columbia and most often used our Westphalia van and later, travel trailer, to set up in the area we were working. This fact greatly pleased our clients, as the cost of doing business in a remote community provided us more funding to work the operational side of the assignment, as we were not required to charge for daily travel costs or local accommodations.

In 1996, I was approached by the Council of International Investigators (C.I.I.), an elite organization of the crème de la crème of investigators world-wide, for membership consideration. C.I.I. headquarters is located in Seattle, Washington and, once accepted and certified as a member of the organization, ongoing training is mandatory. In addition, the annual general meetings are generally held in a different country every year. This part of the membership is amazing, as training courses entail international law, local acts and regulations and the membership resource manual is a beneficial investigative tool for all the members. For example, if a certified member requires assistance on an investigation in another country; a mere telephone call to the country member assures international reciprocity. In that regard, I have worked all over the world as an International Investigator. The credentials are very effective, professionally impressive and greatly circumnavigate international barriers.

Surveillance is an exciting part of investigations and requires a significant amount of skill and patience tempered with common sense: which is exactly what the law requires. Observation of non-verbal communication is the essence of surveillance and criminal case investigations, as words are only seven percent of communication. Being licenced as a private investigator demands the adherence of all regulations and rules that must be obeyed; especially in the heat of the chase: whether on foot, vehicle, bicycle, public transit or boat pursuit. In fact, we have done it all, from floating on a lake acting like young lovers gazing into each other's eyes (while filming the subject), to being bird watchers, golfing, gardening, mobile produce vendors and anything else that got us nearer to the subject or claimant - in our pursuit of evidence and the truth.

My wife has the insight and ability to quickly change clothing, hair style and general demeanor within minutes while on surveillance and can easily defuse a hyper vigilant claimant; thereby obtaining the desired evidence without being discovered.

In British Columbia, privacy legislation regulations were established for a reason. The *Freedom of Information and Privacy* Act legislation works on the premise of what is considered to be a *reasonable expectation to privacy.*

In laymen's language, this means the confidence and expectations of citizens to enjoy the privacy of their home, property and, privacy behind fences, partitions, closed doors and covered windows.

For example, it is illegal to trespass for any reason while conducting investigations or surveillance. Climbing a tree near or on the subject's property and videotaping through a window with blinds partially closed or curtains pulled across a window is a breach of privacy. This is self-explanatory, as an individual assumes that there is an expectation to privacy in those situations.

Each province and territory in Canada has different privacy regulations and it is incumbent on the investigator to know those subtle differences. For example, if an insurance company in Alberta hires a private investigator in British Columbia to conduct surveillance on a former resident of another province who has an injury claim from previous residence in that province, and the evidence obtained does not meet the privacy regulations for the other province, the law firm or insurance company may not be able to use the evidence obtained in British Columbia.

Another example might be where a claimant residing in British Columbia takes their garbage out to the curb and off their property; whereas the investigator can remove the bag of garbage, sort through the refuse and possibly find evidence that discredits the claimant: evidence which may not be admissible in another province. To clarify, British Columbia Privacy Legislation states that when someone discards their refuse on public property, that property is deemed to be abandoned. Dumpster diving is a resourceful tool and has reduced the quantum (exposure) of many insurance or civil litigation cases in our province.

My wife's apprenticeship highlighted these privacy principles. Not all private investigators adhere to those principles - although the Security Program Division of the Ministry of Public Safety details a condition of the *Security Agencies Act* (SSA) on the back of the Security Workers Licence which states: *Must be in compliance with Section 14 of the Security Services Regulation "Code of Conduct."* As a retired government official, I am acutely aware of those provisions and demand as much from company employees.

With numerous case files on our desks at any given time, we usually planned our day the evening before. During a busy period we divided up the current case load and, at first daylight departed the office in separate directions:

unless we were working a file together. Vehicle pursuit is difficult if the claimant or subject is hyper vigilant. Leap frogging: using two vehicles to shadow the claimant generally proves effective in that situation.

The rule in surveillance is to never make eye contact with the subject: as the eyes are the windows of the soul. An eye ping, as it is called in the industry, is when a subject looks into your eyes and subconsciously remembers your face later while actively being pursued.

Earth tone coloured clothing, innocuous coloured vehicles and Sub Rosa (covert) behaviour are critical and necessary for success. A good surveillance investigator can generally spend four to five days parked near a claimant's residence or work place before a subject becomes aware of the surveillance. Parking in front of the subject's house in a bright red van ends the day early, in spite of T.V. shows depicting investigators pursuing a subject in a bright red convertible with the top down.

In the summer of 1998, I applied for a Security Guard Category for our company and being grandfathered as a Security Officer, commenced hiring and training Security Guards through our company; which we renamed Ace Investigations & Security, under the banner of our Incorporation.

Between the years 1998 and 2010, our company was instrumental in acquiring construction security contracts as well as static security work. As our company was a dual category licence and not just security, we made a decision to turn down roving security and only provided static security services to our clients. However; construction security is lucrative and it became necessary to hire security guards for sites requiring twelve to twenty-four hours security a day during construction of commercial buildings. On jobs requiring around the clock security, it became necessary to hire up to 21 security guards. Payroll was huge and if the client paid in arrears, we had to carry a large payroll overdraft. Thankfully, we were successful in obtaining contracts where the client paid us twice monthly, thereby keeping our employees contented. Some of those contracts lasted up to two and a half years providing much needed employment within the community. It was a good run and we enjoyed being able to hire and train local security personnel.

As earlier touched upon, during my military career I had the good fortune to attend numerous Instructional Technique Courses at Canadian Forces Base Borden, and taught in three trades training schools in addition to being employed in the Standards Branch of one of those schools; thereby qualifying in the area of curriculum development, course training standards and classroom presentations in respect of: enabling objectives, performance objectives and classroom presentation. Teaching has always been a passion and I enjoyed training staff to a higher level of professionalism.

After retiring from the military, and while employed with Police Services Branch, I wrote and delivered training program courses during my employment as the Zone Manager, Northern Region, Provincial Emergency Program at which time I was managing 16 Area Coordinators who assisted as emergency program volunteers with fifteen RCMP Detachments within the Prince Rupert RCMP Subdivision. The professional acquaintances and friendships acquired from working with the RCMP were formed for life and became a resource for many years during my career as a licenced private investigator.

Being known and respected by serving police officers is a definite asset while performing the duties of an independent investigator. Those contacts presented opportunities for me to provide police defence work and RCMP Veterans Advocacy.

In 2010, while employing approximately 21 to 23 Security Guards and four investigators, I made an application to the Justice Institute of

British Columbia for a Security Trainers Licence and, upon grandfathering; opened *Ace Training Academy,* operating out of the former Maple Bay Elementary School. With the assistance of my wife Gloria, we put on Basic Security Training Courses (BST 1 and 2) thereby hiring graduating students to work in our security company.

The following true-life crime: criminal, civil, surveillance and investigation cases highlight some of the complexities of the required tasks of licenced private investigators and the importance of the *Charter of Rights & Freedoms*; as related to the criminal justice system.

These factual, and at times humorous anecdotes, are meant to entertain and share some interesting cases that we had the privilege to be involved with over a 26-year period. The names of the subjects and/or claimants have been omitted or changed to protect the innocent and provide due process. In most of these cases, there is a direct relationship between established guilt and guilty knowledge.

It appears that there may be a little larceny in all of us and, it became evident over time that this vice was no respecter of persons; cutting across all lines of age, position, character and socioeconomic status. Our files included men, women, lawyers, doctors, blue collar, white collar, citizens, non-citizens and every walk of life. We were never bored and the work also brought us into contact with persons of the highest values and conduct.

CHAPTER 3

Civil Investigation Case #1

In the fall of 1996, one of our law firm clients hired me to investigate a criminal file which would have most likely turned into a civil claim regarding the alleged assault of a bar patron supposedly perpetrated by the night shift bartender. The purpose of the investigation was to determine the financial exposure to the establishment and, the likelihood of criminal charges against the bar employee. In this case, the bartender was working his last shift of a long career in the industry. In fact, it was his 65th birthday and he was about to retire at the end of the day.

According to the victim (and claimant) who reported to the police that he was viciously assaulted by the establishment's bartender in the alley outside the bar and witnessed by an independent customer; the police opened an investigation. My assignment was to interview the employee and locate any other witnesses who might have seen the assault.

Meeting with the alleged assailant in his

home, the devastated accused male told me that he had been working behind the bar on a quiet evening - the last day of his employment and also his birthday, when a scruffy looking individual came up to the bar and told him that he urgently needed to speak with him outside in the alley. Going out the door, the bartender noticed an adult male lying on the ground with multiple contusions to his face and head. There was blood all over the victim's face and he was moaning and writhing on the ground. As the bartender neared the man lying in a fetal position on the ground, the injured male stated that he did not want his help and that he would take care of himself. Believing that the man was not in any imminent danger, the bartender went back into the bar and continued serving the few remaining patrons until his shift ended.

The accused went on to remonstrate that within a few days after the incident in the alley, he had been charged with assaulting the patron and, that his former employer had hired a lawyer and denied any culpability of the establishment. In essence, the retired employee was being threatened by the bar owner that if there were any financial damages to the establishment, the insurance company would most likely subrogate those damages onto the former employee should he be convicted of assault causing bodily harm.

Immediately upon meeting with the

retired bartender it became obvious to me that he was telling the truth (the absence of guilty knowledge) as he expressed that he had no motivation to assault the unknown male, nor did he personally know the victim or the witness. The description of the victim and the witness was rather vague and unremarkable as it was dark in the alley and he had no idea that he would be charged with assault.

Obtaining a sworn statement from the accused, I reported my observations to the client and recommended, based on the sincerity of the accused, that the client vigorously defend the retired bartender as I was certain that we could prove his innocence.

My client was a well-respected lawyer who relied upon the continued and successful working relationship with the insurance company and, the presumption of innocence of the accused: who we were both prepared to defend.

As an investigative aid, I generally create a wall board for criminal cases so that I can time line and plot the sequence of events from start to finish. This is a snapshot type of board and more clearly puts the investigation into perspective. Also, it keeps me more focused on the consistency of independent statements; with a snapshot view of all the facts.

Having created the crime scene board, I was ready to commence enquiries in the neighbourhood of the alleged victim. We refer to this activity as canvassing and, during the hundreds of criminal investigations that I have conducted over the years, canvassing of a neighbourhood generally renders positive and non-subjective results. Canvassing is also something that major crime investigators undertake at the onset of a criminal investigation, and the procedure that military police investigators (former special investigations unit) conduct while investigating security clearance renewals on serving military personnel and/or senior government officials. It is amazing what can be learned from neighbours, coworkers, local drinking establishments and distant friends and relatives of the subject of the investigation.

Working from a safe location in an imaginary grid around the victims last known address (LKA), I began knocking on doors. The first three enquiries provided very little information and, being careful not to alert the subject, I knocked on a door closer to the subject's LKA residence. To my immediate elation, the homeowner invited me into his doorway and proceeded to tell me about the alleged victim and long-time neighbour.

The contact described the subject as being alcoholic, mean-spirited, lazy and out of work. In addition, he suggested that I should speak with the alleged victim's wife, who lived across the street and was currently separated from her spouse. I took notes and departed the residence. Returning to my vehicle, I pondered whether or not I should interview the estranged wife as generally this is not wise, as it is a well-known fact that a spouse will separate from an abusive partner and for convenience and/or codependent reasons later reconcile with the abuser.

Pondering the situation, I made a decision to knock on the door of the alleged victim's last known address. Standing on the front porch after ringing the doorbell, I was greeted by a young woman in her late twenties to early thirties. Through the open front doorway I noted that there were two elementary age school children in the house. Producing my credentials and enquiring about the subject of my investigation, the lady identified herself as his estranged wife.

Upon learning that I was enquiring about her estranged husband, the mother of two children invited me into her home. Before I could commence a line of questioning, the estranged wife advised me that she was represented by legal counsel, was in the process of a divorce and did in fact have knowledge about the alleged assault.

Pleased that I had arrived at the decision to knock on her door, I enquired as to the name of her lawyer and she provided me his business card. I knew the lawyer and asked if I could call him from her house phone.

The wife and *soon to be witness* agreed and I called her lawyer. He immediately recognized my name and gave me permission to speak with his client on the condition that I ask questions only related to the assault file. I agreed, hung up the phone and gave the new contact my business card which she clipped to a magnet on the fridge door. Near the same place that her lawyer's business card had been placed.

The estranged wife sent the children to a back play room and told me that her husband was unemployed, an alcoholic and, that he recently told her that he had paid an acquaintance five hundred dollars to provide a false statement to the police about the assault by the bartender and, that he anticipated receiving a large financial settlement from the insurance company representing the hotel and bar where he claimed that he had been assaulted. In addition, the alleged victim promised to pay childcare arrears to his estranged wife once he received a settlement. During our conversation, the estranged wife was extremely nervous and begged me not to disclose her name to anyone. Not responding to her request, I obtained her name, address and phone number for the file and departed the residence.

Several hours later after arriving back at our company office, I noticed the telephone answering system LED flashing some messages. The first message was not important; however, the second message was from a female police detective in the city where I had earlier conducted enquires regarding the hotel bar assault case.

The female detective's message was angry in tone and accused me of interfering with her criminal investigation, breaching confidentiality, impersonating a police detective, and obtaining information prejudicial to the Crown's case. The detective's accusations against me were very serious and accused me of conducting enquiries about an ongoing police investigation. Gathering the file notes, I called the detective in an attempt to defend my actions.

The police detective was not receptive to my phone call explanation and expostulated that she had laid a complaint against me with the Director of Security Programs Licencing Branch and was further contemplating charging me with impersonating a police officer and obstruction of justice. I asked for a meeting with the detective and, immediately departed for the police station after calling my client and bringing him up to speed on the accusations of the police detective. What is interesting in this case is that there is no perceived client/solicitor privilege between myself and the client - as I am not the client, only his agent.

As I was required to advise the police that my client was a lawyer and the fact that any questions relating to my client's files had to be directed to the client's solicitor, I informed the detective that I would not be answering anymore questions about the client and that I would immediately come into the police station.

To my benefit, I was fairly well known by the majority of police departments on Vancouver Island and the lower mainland from working with the Vancouver Island and Prince Rupert RCMP Sub-divisions and, consequently, had established a level of credibility over the years.

Upon arrival at the police station, I noted that the watch commander on duty was an acquaintance and asked him to attend with me in the detective division.

The first encounter with the female detective was not pleasant and I was required to endure her wrath for about five minutes before being in a position to defend myself. The focus of the detective's wrath was that she had an open investigation alleging that the subject of my enquiries was being investigated for child sexual abuse.

When the female detective took a breath, I expostulated, in front of a room full of male police officers, that I was in fact working for a law firm, had absolutely no knowledge of the content or subject of her investigation and, that I had clearly identified myself as a private investigator and informed the estranged wife that I was investigating an alleged assault matter. In addition and, while still explaining my involvement, I further told the detective that I had been given permission to speak with the estranged wife's lawyer (whom I named) and that I had observed the estranged wife clip my business card on her fridge door.

Hearing what I had to say and realizing that the watch commander knew me personally, the female detective appeared slightly mollified; thereby giving me the opportunity to tell her that I suspected that the estranged wife had experienced cognitive dissonance after I departed her home, and had consequently phoned her estranged husband and told him, as a means of defending her implied betrayal, that I had deceived her in an attempt to discredit his insurance claim. I further explained that the estranged wife called the police detective to establish credibility with her estranged husband, as she had conspired with her estranged husband to phone the police and lay a false complaint against me; thereby absolving herself from any wrongdoing.

Having successfully cleared up the matter, I left the police station and continued with the investigation. The following day I attended with the police department in the jurisdiction of the alleged assault and advised the investigating officer of the facts that the alleged victim had paid a witness to provide a false statement to the police. The investigating officer was not pleased with the deception of the witness and advised me that he would get to the bottom of the witness statement. Departing the police station, I concluded my file at that time, as it was obvious that the charge against our client would not go forward.

Several weeks later my client, the lawyer who had hired my services, made an application to the court to have the case heard before a judge. At that particular hearing the client presented my affidavit regarding the results of the enquiries and the judge ruled on his application to dismiss the civil suit.

Furthermore, I was told by my client that the judge addressed the alleged victim and told him that not only was he going to dismiss the civil claim against the hotel and former employee, but that he was assessing punitive damages to the tune of $40,000.00 to cover legal expenses related to the alleged victims legal defence costs.

It is relevant to note that insurance fraud is a punishable offence often enforced in the United States, but rarely applied in Canada. However, as a means to minimize insurance fraud, the Insurance Crime Prevention Bureau (ICPB) of Canada maintains a list of insurance fraud cases and employs a number of investigators who work with the insurance companies to effectively compile a list of the names of people who perpetrate insurance fraud. In this case, I advised the ICPB of the results of my investigation, thereby alerting them to the name of the fraudulent claimant and maintaining a working relationship with that organization.

The fact that the judge imposed punitive damages against the alleged victim significantly impacted his solicitor who apparently did not get paid for his legal services. It was also reported by my client that the perpetrator and his co-conspirator were charged with public mischief.

CHAPTER 4

Surveillance Case #1

This surveillance case is about a middle-aged male who was purported to have slipped and injured himself on his landlord's front steps. This type of case is generally a nuisance torte and, depending on the severity of the injuries, can result in compensation for pain, suffering and possibly special damages. This particular case was civil in nature and as often occurs with guilty knowledge, the claimant generally hires a lawyer on contingency, and the lawyer will send a letter to the insurance company (defence or insurer) as a pre-notice for damages. If the insurer denies the claim, the claimant's lawyer has two years (statutory limitation) to issue a Writ (Notice of Civil Claim) and the matter can take anywhere from two to five years to settle; depending of the circumstances of the injuries.

In the case of fraudulent reporting of an injury, the plaintiff (injured party) generally relies on a quick, out of court nuisance settlement. In the matter of the male tenant, he maintained that the fall was quite serious and that he fractured his *left* leg, requiring a plaster cast and, in his statement of claim, proffered that he was unable to work in his profession as a construction worker.

Several days after the injured male hired a lawyer and filed damages, I was retained to provide surveillance on the suspect claimant. There was little known about the claimant; a common evasive strategy at the onset of an impending law suit, and it became necessary to conduct background enquiries; followed by a minimum of three consecutive days of surveillance.

Three consecutive days of surveillance is initially a starting point as it is meant to establish a pattern of the claimant's activities. Some claimants will remain off work (if they are in fact working) for two days, go back to work on the third day, and then claim that they can't work on the fourth day as they are in too much pain from going back to work, thereby attempting to establish that they were trying to mitigate their financial losses and effectively documenting proof of injury.

In a case like this, we escalate surveillance and continue as long as our client wants to pay for investigative costs. As a point of interest, an insurance company notified of an insurance injury claim is required under the *Insurance Act* to place in trust, a financial amount of the anticipated exposure (or quantum as related to case law for that type of injury) until the claim is settled. Of those monies, five percent of the grid exposure quantum can be used for legal and/or investigative services.

For example, if the suspected injury claim damages are established at $100,000.00, the administrative costs could be as high as $5,000.00; which could be an interim fee paid for investigation of the claim.

This is only a guide, and the cost for investigation is generally determined by the defence lawyer in consultation with the insurer (insurance company). In the matter of a severe disabling injury with the potential for a large financial compensation, the investigative costs could be as high as $15,000.00 or $20,000.00.

The background investigation revealed that the claimant was from Ontario and the son of a municipal police chief in a small rural police department outside of Toronto. In addition, it was learned that the claimant was estranged from his family and had provided no witnesses to the alleged slip and fall.

Checking out the address provided by the client, I noted that the alleged injured party lived in a rental property situated along the Gorge Waterway. Reconnoitring the property from a public road, it appeared that the back of the house was approximately 50 to 75 feet from the waterway and that a covered patio was attached to the rear of the bungalow.

Further observation indicated that surveillance was going to be difficult, that it would be necessary to observe the claimant from the rear of the property and, that we would need to conduct surveillance in the tall grass on the bank of the waterway. This fact greatly minimized pursuit capabilities by virtue of the fact that the claimant could exit the front door while the investigator was positioned at the rear of the property.

Attempting to minimize losing the claimant and missing valuable surveillance evidence, I positioned my partner at the end of the street where the claimant resided until such times as I could establish a pattern of movement. There being no activity, we departed the area.

The following morning, we both attended the claimant's residence and, with my partner near the front of the house, and me behind the house near the waterway, I commenced observation on the rear of the residence. My view of the kitchen, back door and patio area was fairly good and I settled down in the grass in anticipation of some activity.

At approximately 12:15 p.m. I observed, on videotape, the claimant exiting the rear patio door of the house with a plaster cast on his *left* leg extending from his knee to his foot. In his right hand the claimant was grasping a walking crutch and a six pack of beer while the other crutch supported his weight. With ease of movement the claimant set the half box of beer on a small table beside the lounge chair, lowered himself to the seat and, having leaned his crutches against the house commenced drinking beer. Having established his routine for the day, I released my partner from her observation position near the front of the house. After drinking four bottles of beer over a period of forty-five minutes, the claimant lay back on the lounge chair and went to sleep. Maintaining surveillance, I obtained a quick clip of tape every hour establishing the claimant asleep on the chair.

At approximately 4:30 p.m. the claimant woke up, looked around and reached over for both crutches leaning against the house, struggled to his feet, picked up the nearly empty beer box and laboriously moved into the house and closed the sliding door.

For two days the claimant exhibited the same pattern of drinking beer and sleeping for several hours on the lounge chair before waking up and awkwardly returning into the house. During those two days, I was able to acquire approximately six hours of videotape of the claimant drinking beer and sleeping on the lounge chair. The weather was warm and dry and surveillance was under optimal conditions. In addition, I was able to observe the claimant in complete obscurity from my position behind some tall grass on the bank of the waterway.

On the morning of the third day, I arrived mid-morning and saw the claimant resting on the lounge chair drinking beer and noticed that the two crutches were leaning against the exterior wall of the house adjacent to the claimants *left* leg.

After obtaining a few minutes of videotape something seemed different from the previous two days. Taking a more detailed look, I noticed that there was no cast on the claimant's *left* leg: the leg facing towards the house on the other side of the lounge chair.

Curious as to why the cast was not on the *left* leg, I repositioned myself where I could better view both of the claimant's legs. Subconsciously thinking this odd, I took photographs of the left leg without the plaster cast. After falling asleep for approximately forty-five minutes, the claimant woke up, looked around in apparent confusion, sat up on the lounge chair and, struggling to his feet, reached behind himself and extracted a Velcro "wrap-around leg cast" from under the lounge chair and proceeded to strap the cast on his *right leg*: the leg on the outside of the lounge chair and closest to my position. The claimant then stood up, looked around again and walked into the house without the aid of the crutches.

Several minutes later he came back outside, retrieved his crutches and walked unimpeded back into the residence. It was obvious at that time that the claimant had inadvertently placed the Velcro "wrap-around cast" on the wrong leg. Securing more videotape and several photographs, I departed for the afternoon.

Reporting to the client the following morning, it was absolutely clear that the claimant had attempted to deceive his lawyer and the insurance company. Based on surveillance observations, my client called the insurer and, through that communication the new evidence was brought to the attention of the claimant's lawyer. Of course, the claimant's lawyer was quite annoyed and embarrassed to learn of the fraudulent claim perpetrated by his client.

Just to be fair to those claimants who are really injured, not all claims are fraudulent; however, if the insurance company or law firm suspects deception, surveillance or investigation is generally warranted.

The fact that this particular claimant exhibited a hyper-vigilant manner and scanned the area before getting up from the lounge chair, and again before walking back into his house without the aid of the crutches on the third day, is indicative of guilty knowledge and a conscious attempt to deceive the insurance company for financial gain.

CHAPTER 5

Criminal Case # 2

This particular insurance file turned into an extensive criminal investigation through uncovering a major crime syndicate involving stolen property; in the form of rare and expensive Swiss watches. It was later in the fall and I was hired by the claims manager of a large insurance company to investigate a theft of an expensive watch that had been reported stolen to the Saanich Police Department and subsequently referred to the insurance company of the alleged theft victim.

After meeting the client, I commenced an investigation into the matter dealing with a "break & enter" of a single-family dwelling. The facts of the case were that the claimant reported to the police that someone had pried open his residence bedroom window, entered the house and stolen a very expensive Day and Date - 40 automatic, 18K gold and diamond jewelled Rolex Swiss watch. Having obtained a police report, the victim filed a loss claim with his insurance broker; at which time he provided a signed statement of claim and written appraisal of the stolen watch for the value of approximately $75,000.00. The claimant also reported that the watch was valued at $90,000.00 new and named the jewellery store where he had purchased the expensive and valuable Rolex.

During a meeting with the subject of the claim (claimant), I was provided a copy of the police report, insurance policy with supporting jewellery schedule depicting the serial number and the appraisal of the watch from a local high-end jewellery store. I immediately recognized the name of the jeweller whose business location happened to be in the Vietnamese district of the city.

My next enquires were with the police, followed by a second viewing of the claimant's home; which indicated pry marks on the exterior of the bedroom window suggesting signs of a forced entry. During this second interview, the claimant was illusive and appeared to be hiding something about the purchase of the watch. Taking photographs of the B & E scene and obtaining a sworn statement from the claimant complete with the name of the seller's store, I proceeded to the jewellery store in question. However, on the way to the jewellery store where the claimant purported to have purchased the watch, I took the opportunity to attend with an Asian friend of mine who owned a watch repair shop in the Chinese part of the city. My friend was extremely knowledgeable and undoubtedly one of the best watch repair technicians on Vancouver Island.

He was a true craftsman, of impeccable character and very well respected in the Asian community. Taking him into my confidence, I shared the facts of the case without breaching the claimants name or the name of the insurance company who had hired me. Upon hearing of the details of the watch, a radiant smile lit up his face and he immediately told me a story about an organized crime gang of fraudulent jewellers who ran late night poker games above the jewellery store.

The contact went on to say that the poker games were fixed and that the unassuming poker players were duped into debt for thousands of dollars as a result of losing poker hands. Having perpetrated a debt in the form of an IOU from the particular patsy, the debt then became unmanageable. Once the debtor was in way over his head, the jewellery store owner began threatening the unsuspecting debtors that if they did not pay off the large gambling debt within a few days, they would most likely be viciously beaten by enforcers and exposed as cheats within the Asian community. Of course, the debtors, usually young men trying to make some money playing poker, became terrified and begged the jewellery store owner for mercy. The scam was large scale and had far reaching tentacles within the Asian community.

The confidential Informant further told me that after threatening the debtor with physical harm, and possibly death, the Asian gang leader; within hours of the impending violent assault, would come up with a solution for liquidating the huge interest accruing poker debt.

The solution to liquidating the debt was that the unsuspecting poker player would be loaned an expensive Rolex Watch and provided a written appraisal in the amount of the poker debt. The appraisal included a description and serial number for the watch. The instructions were that the debtor would take the loaned watch to an insurance broker and initiate an insurance policy with a value amount Jewellery Schedule, return the watch to the jewellery store, wait for approximately 30 days, stage a "break & enter" into their home and report the watch stolen. Obtaining a police report and police file number would then be sufficient evidence to establish the loss of the Rolex and issue a Proof of Claim to the insurer. The money from the insurance claim would pay off the poker debt and the Rolex watch would be available for the next unsuspecting loser.

According to the informant, the watch would make the jeweller hundreds of thousands of dollars; as long as the debtor insured the Rolex with different insurance companies to minimize exposure. Talk about guilty knowledge whereby the debtors feared for their lives and would virtually do anything to get out of the clutches of the organized crime gang.

Learning of the complex fraud scheme, I researched the genesis of Swiss watches made by Rolex and, through another source, learned that it was possible to obtain the selling and buying history of all Rolex watches manufactured in Switzerland. This was exiting news and I obtained permission from my insurance client to proceed with enquires at a prominent Rolex watch making company in Geneva, Switzerland.

On a cold Monday morning in the fall of 1996, I phoned a Rolex watchmaker in Geneva, Switzerland and, after sharing the details of my investigation, the watchmaker agreed to assist me with the background history of the supposedly stolen Rolex. After providing him the details of the watch complete with serial number and where the watch had been sold in Canada, the watchmaker told me to call back in 48 hours.

Two days later, I spoke with the watchmaker a second time. Not surprisingly, he was quite confused about the history of the Rolex watch and told me that I must have been wrong as to where the watch had been purchased; as the records indicated that the watch had been sold to a jewellery vender in Manhattan, New York.

Not to be discouraged, I confirmed the details of the insurance claim and the context of the statement provided by the victim of the theft. The watchmaker was adamant that the diamond jewelled Rolex had been made in Geneva, sold in New York and, that the first owner of the watch unquestionably lived in Manhattan. After considerable wheedling, he provided me with the phone number of the jewellery store that had initially purchased the watch in New York.

The following morning, I called the first registered jewellery store owner of the Rolex and left a message regarding the investigation and the recently learned purchase history of the Rolex as provided through the manufacturer's serial number. I left my email address for his convenience and advised the store that I would be faxing a letter of undertaking regarding the investigation of the watch.

Several days later, I received an email from the jewellery store that initially bought the Rolex from the manufacturer and sold the watch to a client in the Manhattan area and was told that the watch had in fact been stolen from his customer and had never been recovered. In addition, the new contact assured me that he would contact his client in an attempt to locate a police file number and the name of the investigating officer. To my absolute surprise, I received a phone call from the Manhattan jeweller who provided me the name of the investigating detective and the corresponding police file number.

It took several days of phone calls to make contact with the detective who had initially investigated the theft in Manhattan and, after obtaining a police report detailing a full description and photograph of the Rolex, I was able to advise the claimant's insurance company that the insurance claim was fraudulent and that the Vietnamese jewellery store owner was involved in organized crime which was being perpetrated through his jewellery business.

The insurance client provided permission to bring this matter to the attention of the local police department; as private evidence is owned by the insurance client and unless an indictable offence, the file is the property of that particular client. The only exception being if there is a statutory obligation to report a crime. In this case, the client gave me permission to release copies of my investigative report to the fraud section of the local police station and, a full-scale investigation was commenced resulting in the insured claimant being charged with conspiracy to commit insurance fraud and an investigation was opened on the jewellery store.

The watch was eventually returned to the rightful owner in Manhattan.

To clarify classifications of offences, there are three categories of criminal offences in Canada: *summary*, *indictable* and *hybrid* offences (hybrid offences are where the Crown may choose to proceed by either indictment or summary conviction). Hybrid offences cover the majority of the Criminal Code of Canada (CCC) offences.

In addition, Statutory Reporting Obligation imposed by law is the legal obligation to disclose abuse or sexual assault of children; whereby professionals: healthcare professionals, teachers, child welfare workers, social workers, family counsellors, priests, rabbis, or other members of the clergy, operators and employees of day care centers or nurseries, police officers, coroners, victim services workers and other persons in positions of authority who become aware of child abuse. The mandated obligation to disclose also covers a suspicion of the offence, and an obvious non-disclosure will most likely result in a charge against the person, who is by law obligated to disclose.

CHAPTER 6

Surveillance Case # 2

This case is about an insurance file assigned to my wife Gloria to conduct surveillance on a young man 28 years of age who had reported a bodily injury claim to his insurance company as the result of a motorcycle accident.

The initial intake of the file provided full name, detailed description of the subject, address, details of the injury: pre-morbid physical state (any prior injuries at the time of claimed injury) and the fact that the claimant had reported that he was a mechanic claiming loss of employment resultant of the injuries received in the motor vehicle accident (MVA). We were also advised by the insurance company that they had assigned the file to an attorney and that our final report and results of the investigation were to be provided to the client's lawyer. In addition, it was suggested that the claimant had a girlfriend who might possibly be living with him at his last known address (LKA).

Our investigator conducted an initial drive

past of the last known address, made notes of vehicles, motorcycles and other assets at the residence and located a covert place to commence observation on the subject. The initial reconnoitre of a surveillance site is vital to the success of the file.

In the matter of this particular claimant, it was deemed advantageous to observe the rear yard and driveway from an obscure position behind the residence and above the driveway. To be more precise, the back of the property was below a large retaining wall on the street behind the claimant's house; which provided an excellent bird's eye view of the activities in the back yard.

Our investigator backed the surveillance van in against the retaining wall behind and slightly above the subject's residence and commenced surveillance observation from that viewpoint. She immediately noted numerous "big boy's toys" in the yard including a Ducati motorcycle, a Jeep, Seadoo and other vehicles.

Within hours of commencing video surveillance, the claimant appeared in his back yard and was observed working on numerous vehicles of various makes and models. At first it appeared that the claimant was repairing new and older model vehicles. However; within several days it became apparent the subject was working on high end vehicles: mostly

Mercedes, Volvos and new SUV's - obscure coloured vehicles: grey, black and dark silver with limo tinted windows. At that particular time our investigator though it would be beneficial to establish surveillance from the front of the residence for better observation of the claimant's vehicle repair activities.

The mechanical work was steady and there was no shortage of customer vehicles. In fact, it also became evident that the claimant was installing saddle type tanks in the trunk and other areas of the high-end vehicles. It was our investigator's first thought that the tanks might have been vehicle stereo sound boxes.

The majority of the customers were young and of various ethnic origin. As is customary practice, she recorded all vehicle plate numbers, make, model and colour of the vehicles under observation, while also obtaining videotape and still photographs of the vehicles, claimant and his clientele.

Having reached the maximum hours provided by the client for surveillance activities, we were directed to send our evidence and investigative report to the lawyer representing the insurance company. As a point of interest and, as the senior partner of our business, I actively involve myself in every investigation assigned for the purpose of evidence gathering, report writing and submission of evidence to the client. This way, both myself and the investigator assigned to the case maintain full continuity and chain of custody of evidence which would be unassailable in a court proceeding.

Having reviewed over 22 hours of videotape, in addition to the numerous pages of notes taken by the investigator, we became suspicious that the claimant might be involved in a criminal operation and, we made a decision to inform the client's attorney, in writing, that we recommend the file contents be provided to the police. Unfortunately, the client's lawyer, for whatever reason; possibly for the consideration of animus, denied our recommendation and failed to inform the police of our observations.

This decision did not sit well with us; however, our protestations were acknowledged and we were reminded that once our company sold the evidence to our client, the information no longer belonged to our company and became the client's property. To disagree with that decision would most likely be the end of our business as there was no direct or implied *client solicitor privilege* in those particular assignments.

As a point of interest, surveillance activities, especially daily observations over a long period of time usually engenders a psychological relationship between the investigator and the subject, as the investigator is directly involved in the subject's daily life, habits and mannerisms.

In this case, our investigator sensed that the subject was a relatively nice young man with a pretty and respectful girlfriend and was working in order to support his lifestyle choices. However, it was apparent that he walked with a limp and moved around somewhat slowly; which was attributed to the MVA injuries being claimed. Having submitted our evidence and recommendations, we moved on to another file requiring our attention.

Several months after we had submitted our report of the injured mechanic to the law firm with our recommendation that someone call the police, we noticed front page headlines in the local newspaper declaring that the young man and his girlfriend had been brutally beaten with a hammer and stabbed to death in a local motel the evening before and, that the police were soliciting the public for any information leading to the arrest of those responsible for the murders.

It was devastating news to my wife who had concluded the file without knowing if the client had disclosed her evidence to the authorities. In fact, she was very distraught and filled with grief over the death of the nice young couple.

Agonizing over the terrible tragedy befallen the young man and his girlfriend, and in light of the police appeal for public assistance, we phoned the law firm who had been provided our surveillance evidence. Unfortunately, we were promptly told that the evidence no longer belonged to us and that the matter was closed.

Needless to say, we were very disappointed and devised a way to provide the file information to the police without prejudicing our business licence and irrevocably harming the profession of private investigators.

Realizing that the law firm did not intend to disclose the evidence, we made an immediate decision to copy all the evidence tapes; type a list of the description and vehicle licence plate of every vehicle we had recorded and anonymously provide the file to the local police station under the aegis of the *Crime Stopper*s program.

This was a big risk to our company, and could have far reaching affects to our profession. Regardless of the risk, we immediately copied the evidence and listed all vehicles, plate numbers and driver descriptions of those persons who had attended for vehicle repairs. It was a labour-intensive task; however, it was the least we could do for the families of the brutally murdered young couple.

That same evening, I walked into the local police station and dropped several large plain brown envelops on the far end of the counter and walked out. I knew that I had been identified by several of the counter staff in addition to the security camera recording my actions; however, I was determined to make the drop regardless of the consequences.

Within 24 hours the local news reported that the perpetrator had been arrested while trying to flee Vancouver Island. It was a small victory for the families of the victims and a huge break for the police - as the list of vehicle plates and descriptions of the demised mechanics client's would eventually lead to major drug busts over a long period of time. This police operation was code named Operation *"PI", and w*hen questioned by the media about the meaning of the operation's name, the police department responded that *Pi* was the symbol for infinity because the drug trade was infinite; however, we took great comfort in knowing that our evidence had not only led to some justice for the victim's families but had also had a long term impact on the city's drug trade. There was also a rumour that our evidence gathering techniques would be used in future as police training models. We also learned at a later date that the murderer had been sent to settle a drug debt and threatened that if the hit-man did not carry out the murders, his own family would be harmed.

As a retired military veteran and former law enforcement officer, I am acutely aware, through personal experience, of the overwhelming weight and desperation of Post-Traumatic Stress Disorder (PTSD) and in a heartfelt effort to relate to my wife's feelings about the brutal and senseless murder of her surveillance subject and his girlfriend, I can only categorize what is referred to as *a moral injury:* an injury not to the body, not to the mind, but to the inner self, the conscience or moral compass that is deep within ones soul and spirit- unlike PTSD which is a psychological trauma resultant of emotional, physical injury or the fear of impending death. In retrospect, we are grateful to have made a moral decision that resulted in the rule of law.

CHAPTER 7

Criminal Case # 3
Suicide by Police

This particular criminal file was a tragedy to both the police officer and in the death of the perpetrator as a result of his being shot and killed by a female police officer in the line of duty.

Early one Saturday morning in October of 2006, I received a call from a law firm client who required my immediate services to attend at a shooting scene where a male suspect had been shot and killed by an RCMP officer who was his client. This was a very high-profile case and third-party independent evidence was deemed crucial: as there was some doubt whether or not the police officer involved in the shooting used lethal force in the lawful performance of those duties.

Hearing the details of the case, Gloria and I deemed it more beneficial that we work together on the file so that she could obtain photographs of the shooting scene while I commenced an investigation and a canvas for witnesses. At that time, I knew the RCMP Emergency Response Team (ERT) had recently secured and left the scene and had called for an independent investigation by a local municipal police force who, to my knowledge, would not be on scene until the following Monday morning.

Upon arrival at the shooting scene, it was established that there were two parallel west to east apartment buildings in the same complex on either side of a small lane also running east and west between the two buildings. There was a six foot cedar fence on both sides of the lane and I learned that the building manger resided on the second floor on the east side of the building.

Meeting with the building manager proved extremely valuable as he had witnessed the entire event leading up to and including the discharge of firearms; which initially started as an altercation on the Friday evening between the victim and some of the other tenants at around 8:00 p.m. the evening before the fatal shooting at 7:00 a.m. the following morning.

Spending several hours with the witness provided credible background details as to the sequence of events. According to the witness, the deceased tenant lived on the first floor directly beneath the manager's apartment. The manager related that at around 8:00 p.m. the previous night, he received a complaint from two other tenants that the subject was raging outside his apartment door, playing heavy metal music and making threats that he was going to kill the First Nation tenants living near the west end of the building on the second floor of the apartment complex (the apartment several doors west of the manager's suite).

According to the manager, who had had other difficult dealings with the deceased tenant, the tenant was known to vociferously proclaim that he was a member of the Aryan Brotherhood, greatly admired Adolf Hitler, celebrated Hitler's birthday on April 20th and believed that it was his mission in life to rid the nation of non-Aryan people. It was also known by the manager that the subject was supposed to take his anti-psychotic medication and had recently bragged that he was off his medication as it was no longer required.

The manager stated that he called the RCMP around 8:00 p.m. after learning of the threats and hearing the loud music coming from the subject's apartment below and, that two police officers attended later that evening, spoke to the building manager and then pounded on the door of the subject's apartment to no avail, as the heavy metal music was blasting from within. After an hour or so of trying to get the subject to open his apartment door, the police left the property. Several hours later, the manager again called the RCMP

Emergency number and two more officers attended spending most of the night trying to get the subject to open his door.

At around 5:00 a.m. the loud heavy metal music suddenly stopped and, after a short period of silence, the two officers left. Approximately fifteen minutes later, the male came outside his door and started shouting that he was "doing Hitler's job" and was "going to kill the Indians in the building" and then went back into his apartment.

The two police officers, who had only left the property minutes before, arrived back on scene and called the Emergency Response Team who responded minutes later and set up a perimeter surveillance team in an attempt to communicate with the subject, who had again refused to come outside his apartment.

The manager also advised me that one of the other tenants knew that the deceased male did in fact possess illegal firearms in his apartment as he had recently bragged about his arsenal of firearms to other tenants. The manager also said that after nearly two hours of trying to coax the subject out of his apartment, the Emergency Response Team withdrew and the scene was turned over to the responding patrol officers that had arrived prior to the 5:00 a.m. disturbance.

At approximately 7:00 a.m. one of the police officers positioned himself at the north west end of subject's apartment building and the other officer, a female and our client, went around the south side of the building and was approaching the north east side of the subject's apartment when someone yelled that the subject had exited his apartment and was carrying a firearm in his right hand.

According to the building manger, the subject stepped out the door wrapped in a Nazi Flag, turned right (east) and walked to the outside corner of his apartment building. As the subject was turning the corner at the front of the building, the second police officer, (our client), came around the far south front corner, saw the subject and yelled: "Police! Drop your weapon!" This command was shouted several times in rapid succession.

At the same time the other police officer who was positioned at the far west end of the building commenced firing at the subject. The apartment manager stated that he had a bird's eye view of the north east corner of the apartment building where the subject was creeping around the corner in the direction of the other constable.

Looking out his side widow, the street side of the building, the building manager said that he witnessed the female officer come around the south side of the building, issue two more commands and, hearing the gunfire from the other side of the building, fired two shots directly at the subject who immediately dropped to the ground.

He went on to say that the female officer then walked towards the subject and ascertained that he was fatally wounded and called for an ambulance. In the meantime, the female officer began looking for the weapon that she had seen in the subject's hand prior to discharging her service weapon. The scene was cleared several hours later after the weapon was found in the drain beside the front of the building.

After obtaining a taped interview of the building manager's statement, the manager took me on a tour of the property and pointed out the positions of the subject and both police officers at the time of the shooting. For the next several hours my partner obtained photographs while I continued gathering evidence and witness statements.

During one of my interviews, it was suggested that I speak with a certain individual in the building on the other side of the entry lane and, upon attending at that apartment, I was advised by a male, who reluctantly told me that he personally knew the subject, who he had met years before in Ontario. He also said that he knew that the deceased man was going to be shot dead as he had made threats that he was going to kill someone two days before the shooting and that the deceased acquaintance was tired of living in the apartment building with non-Aryan people. The witness also said that he personally saw the guns in the deceased man's apartment and knew that he was dangerous and unpredictable when off his medication.

This was crucial evidence and fully supported the information provided earlier by the building manager. In addition, the witness told me that he had not been interviewed by the police and that he was not going to say anything until someone knocked on his door. I taped his testimony, obtained a hand drawn sketch of the shooting scene and annotated that the deceased male had bragged that he was going to kill someone on Saturday night or Sunday morning. It was good evidence and established a time line prior to the fatal shooting of the violent tenant.

After taking the statement, I continued canvassing the buildings and obtained two other taped statements that fully corroborated the building manager's testimony and the statement of the subject's former acquaintance. For the next several hours my partner and I located numerous bullet holes in the west – east cedar fence.

Returning to our offices we prepared three copies of our findings complete with taped witness statements, photographs and a detailed drawing of the shooting scene. On Monday following the Saturday early morning shooting; I attended with my client and produced the evidence which established that the shooting death of the subject was irrefutably proven to be death by police suicide and self-defence on the part of the policewoman.

Unfortunately, the female police officer resigned from the police force shortly after being exonerated of unlawful discharge of a fireman in the performance of her duty. Sadly, the details of the case became a media circus and several national newspapers decried the police shooting of the male who had been a member of the white Aryan brotherhood cause, which politicized his death. As an independent investigator I find it very difficult to comprehend the castigation of a brave and dedicated police officer in the performance of her duties.

To *Serve and Protect* the residents in our communities is indeed a double-edged sword. My heart goes out to the brave policewoman who made a "fatal" but necessary judgement that particular Saturday morning.

CHAPTER 8

Child Protection Case # 1

As our business success and reputation continued to grow, the demand for our professional services increased due to the quality of our results spread by word of mouth from appreciative clients.

On a warm August morning, the office phone rang and a prominent law firm in the capital city requested that I attend at their offices to discuss a high-profile case involving the protection of a seven-year-old boy. We opened a file and my wife and I attended with the lawyer the following day.

The details of this case led to several other assignments involving small children in need of protection from abusive parent(s) generally relative to child visitation rights. In this case, the child was in the custody of his grandmother; an influential and well-respected business woman in the community. The child's father was the son of the matriarch and the grandmother was our client through the assignment from her law firm.

The case involved 21 days of around the clock observation on the child who was scheduled, through the courts, to have visitation with his mother who lived in another city. To the child's detriment, the mother was known to have been involved with a notorious biker gang and, had lived in another province before losing custody of the child.

In addition to obtaining the full details of the prior abuse, known associates of the mother and the criminal activities perpetrated against the helpless child, my wife and I were provided a blanket apprehension order with strict instructions that if we saw or suspected any physical or emotional abuse or neglect of the child; we had the authority to call the police and apprehend the seven-year-old boy. As the surveillance was 24/7, it became necessary to work with my wife on a 12 hour per day rotation watch.

At approximately 10:30 a.m. on the day of custody transfer, we followed the mother, her child and a male companion, in two separate company vehicles (surveillance van and surveillance SUV) onto a ferry and commenced surveillance at that time. It was a difficult pursuit and remaining obscure was of prime concern.

Exiting the ferry on the lower mainland, we followed our ward to a remote area in a village east of Vancouver and set up surveillance at the address which had been provided to us by the child's paternal grandmother.

Immediately upon commencing surveillance, it became evident that the child, his mother and her male companion were living in a cabin on the edge of an industrial roadway. In fact, there were three cabins on the property and we assumed that the property was owned by the motel on the north side of the cabins.

In an attempt to be respectful of the *Trespass Act* (B.C.), I attended at a local business across from the cabins, identified myself as an investigator and pointed out our surveillance vehicle which happed to be our company Westphalia van and the fact that we were in the area on authorized legal authority and requested that our presence be ignored by the business. Returning to our surveillance van we commenced our first day of observation.

While watching the subject's cabin, we observed the female from the local business walking across the road in the direction of the subject's cabin. With absolute awe, we watched the business person knock on the door of the cabin and, when the mother of the child opened the door, the business female pointed to our van and walked back to the business. We were absolutely shocked at the brazen disregard for our legal reason for being in the area and the danger that she had placed us in relative to the protection of the child. As we had been busted within five minutes of commencing surveillance, I had to move our vehicle out of the area so that my wife could maintain surveillance from behind the motel.

Parking our surveillance van at the far end of the service road, I walked back to the business in question and spoke to the owner. Unfortunately, the owner of the business had no empathy for the dangerous position his employee had placed the child and us in and he was rude and directed that we leave his property. It was evident at that time that the subject had rented the cabin during the 21 day visit from the business we had spoken to earlier that morning.

Conducting surveillance around the clock proved difficult as we had to continually move the surveillance vehicle during daylight hours as our cover had been disclosed in addition to the purpose of our attendance in the area.

The third morning of surveillance proved quite difficult as just prior to daylight we saw the boy's mother's boyfriend walking on the road looking for our surveillance van. Banging on the door of our van, the male said: "Hey Mr. PI, I know you're in there, would you like a coffee?" It was extremely difficult and I remained silent, although I wanted to confront him which would have confirmed that someone was in fact in the vehicle. Tinted windows and curtains all around the van proved a definite asset. The male left after a few minutes and I was able to obtain a photograph of him as he walked away.

When my shift was over and my wife took over surveillance, I proceeded to the local police department, established who I was, explained the case we were working on and our authority to apprehend the child with the assistance of the police. The watch commander was extremely co-operative and when I showed him the picture of the male who had banged on my vehicle door earlier that day; he identified him by his full name as a prospect for the biker gang. The officer disclosed that the subject male had a criminal record of child abuse. It was good information and I provided a copy of my credentials and the apprehension order, should an intervention become necessary.

The following afternoon, while watching the subject's cabin from the street several hundred feet south of the cabin, I heard the ominous rumbling of a Harley Davidson motorcycle slowly riding past my surveillance van. The Harley stopped approximately two hundred feet down the road, turned slowly and faced my vehicle. The man on the bike was huge and wore the insignia of his biker gang. Not only was he huge, but he wore a Viking horned skull cap on his head and his entire face was a shaggy mass of red hair and beard. He was most ominous.

The daunting male gunned the throttle and stared in my general direction as the bike inched slowly forward. Every few feet he would stop the bike, place his boots on the ground and give my vehicle, which was facing towards his position - the thousand-yard stare. It was annoying, intimidating and a perceived threat. He kept edging closer and closer and the intense stare of the huge male became more and more disconcerting.

Thinking that I was going to be beaten to death and tossed into a barrel filled with concrete, I became resolved to remain where I was regardless of the imminent danger. My job was to protect the child and that was what I was prepared to do; regardless of the consequences. Looking through the front curtain of the van, it was indeed evident that the biker was wearing his club colours and slowly moving towards my surveillance vehicle.

Several minutes later, I observed the bike creeping closer and closer to my vehicle. As he was directly alongside my van, on the driver's side of the vehicle and, as I was facing northeast, he stopped and placed his huge black biker boots on the ground.

Speaking through the outside wall of my Westphalia van I said, "I know who the male is in the house with the child and his mother and you should know that he is a convicted child abuser. My understanding is that your gang does not tolerate child abuse."

After a slight pause, the biker lifted his feet, accelerated quickly and rode away. I knew that he would not come back as he had heard the details of our assignment. Departing to a less visible location, my partner relieved me as my shift was over for the day.

Several hours later, as I was returning to the surveillance area in our company SUV, I noticed an adult female dressed in coveralls painting the front door of a former motel which had been converted into a six-plex rental unit. The motel was directly beside the subject's cabin and situated west to east whereby the back of the motel faced north into the front yard of subject cabin. It was ideal for covert surveillance and, approaching the woman painting the door, I enquired if the owner was on the premises. The female replied that she was the owner and that the suites would not be ready for another few weeks. I sensed immediately that the woman was trustworthy and, in as vague a manner as possible, asked her if she would rent me one of the empty rooms for approximately three weeks.

After a few minutes of chatting, she agreed to rent the one-bedroom apartment for 18 days; as she was completing renovations on the outside and did not intend to rent the Units until the following month.

She took me into the motel room that would facilitate surveillance and, it was perfect. In fact, the bedroom window viewed the porch of the cabin which faced out towards the road at the front of the motel providing a full view of the side and front yard. The owner accepted six hundred dollars cash, we shook hands and I confirmed that no furniture would be moved into the suite.

All she knew was that I was an investigator on authorized business and that my partner and I would be rotating shifts over the rental period. It was an ideal arrangement and upon securing the room, receiving a key and exchanging phone numbers, I departed the area to buy some groceries.

At the end of my partner's shift at 6:00 p.m., I called Gloria's cell phone and told her to drive away from the area, circle back onto the street and park the van two blocks north of the motel located beside the claimant's property and, that I currently was in unit # 4 setting up a tripod for the surveillance camera.

While watching the subject's cabin from

the motel window, Gloria arrived and we brought in our bed from the van and set up the video camera in the back bedroom window and commenced surveillance on the subject's cabin.

Knowing a retired military police friend in the area, I took the surveillance van to his place and he drove me back to the motel in his vehicle. As the subjects had not seen our SUV at any time before, it was ideal to have the vehicle at the motel should we need to pursue the subject and the child on foot or, if necessary in the SUV.

By the following morning, it was evident that the subject and her boyfriend thought we had been chased out of the area. However; knowing this, we ratcheted up surveillance from the motel and started videotaping the chid playing in the front yard. That evening my wife observed the mother, on videotape, brazenly shaving the child's head bald while he was sitting on a chair in the front yard. This was contrary to the court instructions that the child was to have his head covered while outside as he was allergic to the sun. Around noon on the following day, we observed the child exit the cabin with no hat on his head. He appeared distraught and we captured the evidence on video tape.

Contacting the child's grandmother, we relayed the recent head shaving incident. According to our client who called us back in fifteen minutes, the subject's lawyer had immediately called the mother of the child we were watching and told her that the terms of the visitation were that her son's head had to be covered while in the sun.

Within minutes of making the call, we observed the mother and her boyfriend hurriedly walking the neighbourhood looking for our surveillance van. They appeared confused and perplexed which gave us our first positive edge in the difficult surveillance operation.

For the next two weeks we followed the mother and child on foot all over the area. The mother was absolutely hyper-vigilant and there appeared to be no more evidence of abuse as the child's head was covered with a bandanna. Several days after the phone call to the child's mother, we watched and heard the boyfriend being told by the boy's mother to leave the property. It was a successful surveillance operation, and we followed the child back to his grandmother who was waiting at the ferry terminal on the afternoon of the 21st day.

Several years later, we were contracted to provide surveillance on several other high-risk children who were suspected of being abused. It was rewarding work and the courts applauded us for the success of our surveillance operations. In fact, during one of the later surveillance cases my wife's testimony in court resulted in her being designated a Supreme Court Expert Witness.

CHAPTER 9

Criminal Case #4

This criminal second degree murder conviction Appeal file actually came about from my previous employment as a Provincial Corrections Officer while working as a guard in a maximum security institution.

In the late 1980's, I was working in the Vancouver Island Regional Correctional Centre (VIRCC) in Saanich, B.C. The facility was classified as a maximum security institution as it housed a remand centre within the two years less a day classification of sentence. Originally, the jail had been a west wing, east wing open incarceration concept, wherein the inmates, generally a population of one hundred and seventy at peak times, were housed in co-mingled units either side of each other on the second floor. There was also a protective custody unit on the third floor of the original castle, which had been an insane asylum in the nineteen forties and fifties.

As a point of interest, in 1984, after a hostage taking incident in the infirmary whereby a prison guard (whom I had gone to school with at Cowichan High in Duncan) was shot, wounded and left bleeding on the floor of the infirmary in a hostage taking situation during the time that the Senior Corrections Officer (SCO) was being held hostage at knife point.

The hostage situation was resultant of two males being incarcerated after being arrested for shooting and killing a man and his wife in Duncan, B.C. and, while they were awaiting trial, a loaded handgun was smuggled into the prison through a mattress exchange program. The hostage taking was affected through the medical infirmary where the first guard was assigned escort of the prisoner and responding to the hostage taking, the SCO, a former British Commando, was also taken hostage. During the hostage taking event, my school friend was shot point blank in the chest and, turning precisely at the same time as the shot was fired, the bullet entered his left arm above his elbow. Knowing that the wound was not fatal, the injured guard wisely dropped to the floor and lay in his blood without moving. The responding SCO was taken hostage at knife point and the two inmates proceed to load up on drugs from the infirmary.

The following day, the main perpetrator of the hostage taking incident was shot and killed by the police. Fortunately, the guard who was shot in the arm and the SCO survived the ordeal and the prison was rebuilt as a result of a public inquiry through the Standards Branch of the Ministry of Corrections under the authority of the Solicitor General.

After that incident, VIRCC was completely rebuilt between 1984 and 1985. In that reconstruction, the institution was upgraded to a living unit concept where each living unit had one officer and 28 inmates: each inmate housed in separate cells on a two tier floor plan. It was ideal as a provincial prison and the remand unit, during my tenure, was housed in D Unit.

While working in the Remand Unit, I was temporarily assigned to Protective Custody (PC) on the upper deck of the institution. The PC Unit was designed to protect inmates who had been charged and/or sentenced with sexual offences or offences where an inmate required special handling due to the nature of the charges; especially if they were a witness as well as complicit in the crime or offense.

It was during those three weeks of duty in the PC Unit that I first made contact with an inmate awaiting trial on a manslaughter charge. The inmate was a professional artist and spent most of his day painting landscapes and forest scenes.

Through permission of the warden, I was

able to get painting supplies outside the institution for the inmate and we established a mutual understanding of each other; although he knew and understood that I was the guard and that he was the inmate. Respecting the inmate's abilities as an artist and the gentle nature that he presented, I also made arrangements for an Evangelical pastor friend to be placed on the visitors list of the inmate.

Several years later, after being promoted and moving to Police Services Branch, I learned from my pastor friend that the same artist had been sentenced to federal prison for a term of fifteen years for killing his girlfriend on a couch in the alley behind a music store. The details of the case as relayed to me through the pastor, revealed that the artist had been drinking wine on a couch in the alley with his girlfriend, had drunk to excess and passed out during the warm summer evening. Awakening in the morning, he found his girlfriend dead on the couch beside him and a bloody brick on the ground which had been used to beat her to death.

As a former corrections officer and licenced private investigator, I regularly obtained permission to interview inmates in either provincial or federal institutions in North America as I was pre-screened by those institutions whether in Canada or the United States. Those credentials were a definite asset to my clients, as I merely needed to contact the institution and provide my name and former badge number for clearance.

In this particular case, I was granted access to the federal institution and met with the inmate and learned that he had recently applied for an appeal and asked if I would be willing to work with his lawyer. I agreed and made contact with his criminal defence lawyer who immediately recognized my name and contracted my services.

The time was short and we needed to gather sufficient evidence to show mitigation of the charges. The biggest factor to the imprisonment was that the inmate did not plead innocent of the crime of killing his girlfriend as he told the court that he had no memory of the evening in the alley. In fact, he refused to plead not guilty based on the fact that he had had an alcoholic black out and woke up to find his girlfriend dead beside him on the couch. It was a difficult investigation as the convicted man had no defence of his alleged crime.

Several weeks earlier, the defence lawyer was able to obtain supervised bail for the convicted client and he was moved into a shelter up island and, during my initial enquiries, I was able to meet with him and go over the entire case from his initial arrest to the court's sentence. It was during one of those casual meetings in his temporary residence, that I learned the name of a potential witness who might be of assistance in the Appellant Court. Unfortunately, I was unable to locate the witness.

For the next several days, I spent 12 to 14 hours a day interviewing anybody who might have any knowledge of the incident. I must have handed out fifty business cards in the hope of finding someone who could exonerate our client.

At approximately 5:30 p.m. on a Friday afternoon, the end of a very long week of working on the case, I closed my investigators notebook and headed home for the evening. I was exhausted and prayed for divine intervention.

While on the way home my cell phone rang and I heard a message that changed my client's life. Pulling over and stopping the vehicle, I answered the phone and the following conversation took place: "Are you the private investigator who is asking questions about the murder?" With eager anticipation I responded:

"Yes, I am that person. How may I help you?"

The voice was female and she immediately told me that her boyfriend had recently died from a long and painful battle with lung cancer and, that before he died, he uttered a deathbed confession as follows:

"I killed his girlfriend and want the truth known before I die."

She further gave details of the killing which were verbatim as to the facts of the death of my client's girlfriend and subsequent details of the trial. It was compelling evidence and I made arrangements to meet her within the hour.

Attending with the young woman, I took her sworn statement and contacted our client's lawyer. It was the perfect end to a hopeless case and, in trial the following month our client was found not guilty and immediately set free. Prayers were indeed answered.

As a point of interest, I have been hired to assist two other murder convictions on appeal and, I am humbled to say that all of those convictions were overturned and innocent people walked out the gates of federal prisons. I often think of the odds whereby one wrongfully convicted person is spared a lengthy prison sentence and yet, three have crossed my path over the past 25 years. All I can think of in that regard is that those cases were the result of *divine intervention*.

During the many years and hundreds of

criminal investigations that I have been involved with, there were times when I was hired to defend horrible and brutal murder cases whereby the client was in fact guilty. Two of those female murder cases are well known in the province of British Columbia and, I am confident that those persons were guilty and belonged in prison. Even with time served and parole, families were irrevocably changed. Those two cases were the brutal murder of Reena Virk and Rhonda Haynes.

Something that I did not know at the time of working with defence counsel in the latter murder case, was that Rhonda Haynes's father had served with my mother at RAF (Royal Air Force) Station in Gatwick, Sussex, England during the Second World War and, I later realized, that I had made his acquaintance when I was a lad of about 14.

It was devastating and I often regret having had to defend Rhonda's murderer. On the reverse side of that coin is the fact that I was able to free three innocent men from wrongful convictions; which definitely balances the scales for the other two righteous convictions.

CHAPTER 10

Intro to Fire & Explosion Investigations

For centuries fires onboard Naval Ships have proven catastrophic, as there is nothing more devastating and destructive than an onboard fire on a warship as the hull is made of steel and below deck compartments are like metal tombs; with the only means of ingress and egress being through a small watertight hatch. A modern naval ship is designed that way to maintain watertight integrity and, a fire in a dark and smoky compartment needs to be overhauled and suppressed as quickly as possible. Not to forget the horror of crew members being in the compartment when fire breaks out.

On the early morning of October 23rd, 1979 at approximately 0810 hours, Her Majesty's Canadian Ship *HMCS Kootenay* (DDE 258), a Restigouche Class Destroyer Escort; exploded and caught fire approximately two hundred miles off the west coast of the English Channel during a Canadian task group exercise: when *HMCS Kootenay* was ordered to steam full speed ahead (approximately 5,750 rpms). Within minutes of reaching maximum rpm, the reduction gear box overheated and exploded. Seven crew members were killed immediately, two died later and fifty-three crew members were injured. After the explosion, the ship's company was evacuated to the Aircraft Carrier *HMCS Bonaventure* (Home Port Shearwater, Nova Scotia).

The cause of the fire was directly related to the disintegration of the starboard propulsion reduction gear box, located in the engine room directly below the chief & petty officers' cafeteria. It was devastating and reports of the incident memorialize how there was a huge explosion, clouds of smoke and a fire ball that ravished down the Burma Road Flats (main deck fore and aft passageway beneath the quarterdeck), raced past the wheelhouse, officers' quarters, shot up the wardroom hatch in search of more oxygen from the open hatchway on the port side of the upper deck; aft of the ship's Citadel (The Citadel is the Nuclear, Biological Chemical Warfare structure that begins on the quarterdeck and extends to the front of the bridge, creating a sealed above deck fortress). To further add to the confusion, the wheelhouse filled with smoke and the after upper deck hatch in the main cafeteria was not accessible for evacuation.

It was later determined that the reduction gear box, a huge gear box that housed the main propeller shaft system: a gear box that is used to adjust revolution speed had overheated and blown up as the gear had been replaced backwards during the previous refit in Halifax Harbour.

The investigation and Board of Inquiry of *HMCS Kootenay's* explosion led to numerous remedies apropos the spread of the fire, as it was determined that a number of precautions could have minimized the devastation to the crew and ship at the time of the explosion.

As the reduction gear heated up in temperature and the stress on the bearings reached a critical point, the gear box blew out and a fire ball travelled to the deck above; which happened to be the main interior deck of the ship (referred to as Burma Road).

The spread of the fireball was significantly enhanced by the fact that the top deck hatchway, a stairway hatchway accessible from the main cafeteria on the port side of the ship, was open on the upper deck; which provided an immediate source of oxygen to fuel the fireball racing through the ship from the engine room deck below.

The location of the chief & petty officer cafeteria is near the middle of the ship on the starboard side approximately one hundred and eighty feet from either end of the vessel. The other deck hatch, which is forward of the mortar well, is located between the Canteen and Eight Mess. That hatch, plus a doorway hatch in the forward part of the mortar well were closed thereby creating the need for a new source of oxygen supply: which happened to be the forward hatch on the port boat deck. It was unfortunate that the port boat deck hatch to the quarterdeck was open as death and injury might have been greatly minimized.

As a form of remediation for the problem with the portside boat deck hatchway, all DDE's (Destroyer Escorts) were fitted with a *Kootenay* Hatch: a flapper type hatch that immediately seals if fire breaks out below decks. It was a costly situation and we painfully remember our comrades who lost their lives onboard *HMCS Kootenay* that fateful day.

In 1982, the British Warship *HMS Sheffield* was struck broadside by a French Exocet missile during the Falklands War. The missile raced approximately 12 feet above the surface of the sea and impacted with the *Sheffield* amidships. The explosion was witnessed as a bright flash, a large fireball and an implosion of the hull. Many lives were lost as the type of aluminum used in the construction of the warship melted under the intense heat. It was thought provoking and changed naval warfare.

The only difference between the fire on *HMCS Kootenay* and similar fire and implosion of *HMS Sheffield*, was the fact that the first fire and resultant deaths were during a peacetime naval exercise and the second fire and resultant deaths were during an armed conflict. However; both crews experienced catastrophic and fatal results.

During my 12 years of Sea Time (24 hour days logged at sea) in the Royal Canadian Navy (the remainder of my time served in military land establishments), shipboard fires were a constant threat and, every sailor, from Basic Training to Sea Duty were regularly trained in shipboard firefighting.

In that regard, fire drills are conducted daily onboard every ship in the navy. The dreaded pipe (main broadcasting system from the bridge) was preceded by a shrill tweeting of the Bosuns' pipe followed by the words: "this is a drill: fire, fire, fire, fire in the ___; Attack Team muster in the ___." Or conversely, the dreaded words: "This is not a drill: fire, fire, fire - fire in the ___; Attack Team muster in the ___."

Every sailor onboard a Canadian naval vessel is trained in firefighting regardless of rank, trade or department. Fire attack team leaders are generally senior ratings and the Petty Officer of the Watch or Petty Officer of the Day (POW at sea and POD in port) controls the first response team before the hull technicians and engineers close up for fire main and damage control duty.

My professional firefighting career began on my first naval ship in 1966: a Second World War Frigate sailing out of Halifax, Nova Scotia. For a period of 12 years, while at sea during various postings, I was trained in shipboard firefighting duties while ashore at the damage control school at Peggy's Cove, Nova Scotia and Damage Control and Fire Fighting School at Colwood, British Columbia and, onboard ship; which significantly motivated me to earn my fire causation credentials after retiring from the Navy. It was an ideal situation, as rarely fire causation investigators have the experience acquired from shipboard firefighting. The training in the fire schools is extensive and generally entails a three-week course where every crew member is taught how to attack and suppress fires in dark, smoky metal compartment tanks sitting above ground at the land-based school. Senior ratings: petty officers and above are required to train for three weeks and, I personally trained on both coasts as a senior rating.

Shortly after opening our investigation business, I began working fire scenes as a security officer; although sufficiently trained in fire investigations. Within a year of fire scene security duties, a Victoria City Fire Investigator,

Myles Anderson became aware of my Navy training and experiences and invited me to join him on some fire scenes. That encounter and our immediate friendship launched my career as a civilian Fire Causation Investigator.

Through Myles' amazing tutelage, I joined the Canadian Association of Fire Investigators (CAFI) and became certified as a Fire Causation Investigator. It was the beginning of a new career branch as a causation investigator and I worked hundreds of residential and commercial fire scenes between 2001 and 2013, and temporarily left the profession to work as a Pension Disability Officer and Advocate with Veterans Affairs Canada.

The National Fire Prevention Manual - NFPA – *Guide for Fire and Explosion Investigation* was developed by the Technical Commission on Fire Investigations to assist in improving the fire investigation process and the quality of information on fires resulting from previous investigations. The guide is intended for use by both public sector fire department employees who have statutory responsibility for fire investigations and private sector persons conducting investigations for independent companies for litigation purposes (NFPA 921).

The training and certification required for fire and explosion causation is a complex and difficult achievement and, having a military background as a shipboard firefighter greatly enhanced my certification through the Canadian Association of Fire Investigators.

Being part of that organization afforded me the opportunity to join, as a professional fire investigator, the International Association of Arson Investigators (I.A.A.I.) and the Insurance Bureau of British Columbia.

Fire Scientology is the study and application of past, current and future fire and explosion events. When first involved with shipboard firefighting, over 54 years ago, we were taught that the fire triangle consisted of fuel, oxygen and ignition.

However; with the ever-evolving study of fire scientology, we now know that there is a fourth element which refers to the *tetrahedron* (four elements) as being Fuel, Heat, Oxidizing Agent and Uninhibited Chemical Chain Reactions. Years of fire scene experience has progressed to an understanding whereby fire and explosion investigators learn that every natural or man-made material has an ignition point, flash point and fire progression path.

This scientology requires a complex training progression and fire investigators learn the methodology, fire science, fire patterns, fire modeling systems, electricity and fire, building fuel gas systems, fire-related human behaviour, legal considerations, safety, sources of information, planning the investigation, recording the scene, physical evidence, origin determination, cause determination, failure analysis and analytical tools, explosions, incendiary fires, fire and explosion deaths and injuries, appliances, motor vehicle fires, wildfire investigations, and management of major investigations.

The scientific method is to recognize the need (identify the problem, define the problem, collect data, analyse the data, develop a hypothesis, test the hypothesis by deductive reasoning) and adopt the final hypothesis.

As a fire investigator, when I have completed the scientific method of fire investigation and have thoroughly tested and selected a final, indefensible hypothesis, I am then ready to make a decision that is irrefutable (or should be) so that if and when I am questioned or challenged on the witness stand as to how I arrived at those conclusions; I am able to defend this determination by virtue of the fact that I have attacked my own hypothesis which ideally should withstand rigorous cross examination.

It is thought provoking and quite remarkable to see a Fire Causation Investigator on the witness stand being asked by a defence lawyer: "Is it possible, and did you consider that the fire may have been caused by a faulty electrical circuit and not as your evidence suggests?"

A response to that question would invariably be: "No, because I ruled out electrical cause when I conducted an electrical circuit beading test: a system of microscopic examination of copper wiring whereby beading appears on the wire when there has been an arc fault; as copper wire will bead at approximately 1780 degrees Fahrenheit. Further examination of the electrical copper wire, and analysis of the multi-breaker, exhibited no microscopic beading along the wiring - which supports the conclusion that the point of origin, point of ignition and fire progression evolved at a lower temperature; thereby ruling out an electrical arc fault as a source of ignition."

In addition, before scrutinizing the electrical wiring, a cursory examination of the breaker box generally will indicate if the breaker tripped before the arc fault. This fact would further be supported by the evidence of soot being on the inside of the thrown switch (the side that had been on the right side of the switch prior to tripping to the left).

As every hydrocarbon (polymer or molecular structure) has an ignition factor (the temperature where the flammable material will ignite), it is scientifically possible to determine the source of fuel, ignition point and temperature of combustible materials. From that process also comes fire progression, pyrolysis (the chemical decomposition of a compound into one or more other substances by heat alone: pyrolysis usually precedes combustion), better explained that a primary ignition point can produce heated gases which combust and a secondary ignition is produced, resulting in a flashover situation where a low burning fire will roll over a ceiling and cause secondary burning.

There are only four classes of fire causes: accidental, natural, incendiary, and undetermined. Whenever the cause cannot be proven, the proper classification would be *undetermined.* The Fire Investigation Manual states that: *"Any determination of fire cause should be based on evidence rather than on the absence of evidence; however, when the origin of a fire is clearly defined, it is occasionally possible to make a credible determination regarding the cause of the fire, even when there is no physical evidence of that cause available. This finding may be accomplished through the credible elimination of all other potential causes, provided that the remaining cause is consistent with all known facts." (Extract NFPA 921 Guide for Fire and Explosion Investigations 2011 Edition).*

After certifying as a Canadian Fire

Investigator and continuing with various other courses on fire, explosion and vehicle fire investigation; our business clientele changed significantly. Highlighted next are some of the more notable fire scenes that we investigated between 2001 and 2013.

CHAPTER 11

Fire Investigation #1

Two days before Christmas of 2001, I was called by the claims manager of a large insurance company who required my services to investigate a motel/pub fire that had resulted in major structural damage to the building. He stated that the local fire department found the burn patterns on the exterior of the east pub wall suspicious and, the insurance company wanted to know the cause of the fire.

On Christmas Eve day, I attended the fire scene, identified myself by producing my credentials to the security guard and signed the log book before commencing an extensive examination on the exterior of the building. The fire scene was taped off with green and black tape strung around the entrance to the fire scene and the words: "Crime Scene – No Admittance" was written on the tape. I asked the guard if the building had been certified as safe for the purpose of my investigation and he responded that the there was a note in the log affirming that fact.

After a walk around the building, I noted where the fire appeared to have spread from the exterior into the pub lounge. Fire investigation protocol requires that we start with the least fire damage first and then progress to the heaviest damage last (if possible), which generally indicates a point of origin and possibly a source of ignition. Entering the building, it was noticeable that water damage was significant as a result of fire suppression. In addition, the low burning fire had caused flashover (flames rolling over the ceiling) resulting in fire advancement causing significant damage to the inside lounge and east side door entrance. The pub ceiling was dripping wet and the main lounge had been completely burned out from the progression of the fire which was fully involved when the fire department arrived.

The local Fire Commissioner has the legal right to determine if the building is dangerous and/or unsafe to enter or, conversely is structurally sound. Knowing the structure to be reasonably safe, I moved from the least damage to the worst damage in an attempt to locate the origin of the fire. Locating the main electrical box, I determined that the fire had not been started by an electrical arc fault and ruled out that classification. A further examination of the kitchen indicated that the fire had started near the outside kitchen wall on the east side of the building. Exiting the east side door from the lounge, I noticed that there was no evidence of fire damage to the motel rooms which were on the perimeter of the east side of the parking lot.

Returning to the point of ignition, on the exterior of the building adjacent to the kitchen and partway to the door of the lounge, I commenced a more thorough examination of the burn patterns on the exterior walls. The building was of wood construction with horizontal cedar siding on the exterior. As arson is the only criminal charge that requires motive, opportunity and a direct physical link to the fire scene; circumstantial evidence is not sufficient in itself to lay a charge of arson.

For insurance purposes, the determination of arson, where there is no known suspect, is an opportunity for the insurance company to settle with the insured: unless there is criminal negligence causing injury or death as a result of the fire.

Should that be the case, the scene becomes a crime scene and the jurisdiction is that of the Fire Commissioner and local law enforcement. In British Columbia all structural fire scenes come under the authority of the Fire Commissioners Office. As the responding fire chief is deemed to be the Local Fire Commissioner (LFC), authority is given to the LFC and/or Criminal Investigative Section of the policing agency.

While conducting a secondary examination of the area near the interior kitchen (east) wall and, what I considered to be the exterior fire breach from the point of ignition, I was approached by an East Asian female, approximately 45 year of age, who identified herself as the owner of the establishment. She seemed distrustful, visibly distracted, exhibited guilty knowledge and demanded to know who I was and why I was in her building. Presenting my credentials, I immediately began asking questions regarding the fire. I was not surprised when she refused to speak about the fire and gave the excuse that she was busy trying to clean up the bar area. I told her that she was not permitted to be in the building as the fire department had ruled the structure unsafe other than for investigative purposes. We arranged to meet later as I wanted to obtain a written statement. She was unresponsive and her behaviour was odd, and I made notes regarding her attitude, demeanour, and aggressive body language, lack of communication and strong presence of guilt. Most fire damage claimants are generally cooperative with the insurance company and their representatives as they are eager to settle the matter and get back to business.

In that regard, the Insurance Act states that a claimant has fifty-seven days to provide a signed Statement of Loss; before they are entitled to sue for breach of contract. Conversely, once a claimant signs a Statement of Loss, they are placing themselves in a position of scrutiny, as the Statement of Loss is a vital investigative tool as any untrue statements invariably become a matter of record and could cause a denial of full compensation to the claimant.

Refreshing the client's notes from the fire departments observations, the claimant's expostulation and evasive attitude supported the fact that she had recently renovated the premises, re-insured the building at a much higher value and, within several months of reopening the bar encountered a huge fire loss. Re-insuring is also an indication of possible fraud as the owner will inflate the renovation costs and insure the premises at a much higher value. Re-insuring is also a means of establishing loss of business opportunity.

After doing a cursory examination of the fire scene, resultant fire damage and location of the most extensive damage, I left the scene and told the security guard to allow no one in the building without permission of the RCMP and/or myself. After leaving the scene, I attended with the local fire department and obtained a chronological list of the fire report, response time and initial observations of the fire crew.

The meeting at the fire department was a fruitful endeavour and the fire captain confirmed my suspicions that the fire had been deliberately started and that the area of ignition was at the east side of the building, adjacent to the motel laundry room: a stand-alone building attached to the motel but separate from the pub. It was a starting point and my focus would be looking for witnesses and to establish a source of ignition.

Over the next 24 hours I sifted through the fire scene, took hundreds of photographs, drew a fire model chart of the scene, collected samples, checked the electrical panel and secured evidence for the chain of custody of samples and material collected at the point of ignition (burn patterns, evidence of an accelerant and charring of the wooden beams and ceiling joists). After finishing with the scene, I met with several witnesses and obtained statements from staff and patrons.

During one of those interviews, a patron named a witness whose family name I recognized from going to school with several of his relatives. Making a quick phone call provided the phone number for the witness and he agreed to meet in the parking lot of the fire scene.

While interviewing the witness: the younger brother of my school friend, he told me that he had been sitting in the restaurant side of the bar beside a window at the time of the fire and witnessed a chambermaid: an Asian female in her late twenties; running across the parking lot with a ten litre red plastic fuel container - minutes before the outbreak of fire.

The witness described the woman as average height, medium weight and wearing blue jeans, running shoes and sweatshirt and had dark hair covering most of the sides of her face.

The time of that incident was recalled as being around five o'clock p.m., two days before Christmas. I asked the witness if he had spoken to the police or fire department, or for that matter, anyone else; and the witness responded that he had not wanted to get involved.

Explaining that it would be in his best interest to provide a written statement, before the police found out that he was avoiding communication, he agreed to provide a statement which was secured on my camcorder. Before he left, I advised him to maintain silence about the statement but that he was to contact the local police and advise them that he had provided me with a taped statement.

Prior to speaking with the witnesses, I had determined that an accelerant had been used as a source of ignition and fire enhancement and, in that regard, had obtained a sample of the hydrocarbon liquid residue using a chromatography meter (used extensively in forensic science) to identify the accelerant. The witness's statement conclusively established that the fire had been deliberately started.

Having obtained the sample and completing the chain of custody evidence document certifying that there had been no cross contamination of the sample, that the sample had been placed in a sealed evidence container (sterilized paint tin), that I had marked the sample container with my initials, date and file #, and sent the sample by courier to the RCMP Forensic Unit.

It is crucial that chain of custody of the sample evidence be documented from hand to hand so that a defendant attorney can't claim that the chain of custody was breached and make a motion to the court that the evidence be ruled inadmissible. Contaminated or mishandled evidence is the number one reason criminal cases are usually dismissed by the courts.

While working inside the heavily damaged bar, an East Asian male approximately 50 years old walked into the building and stood inside the door. As I approached the male, he appeared extremely nervous, hyper-vigilant and, when asked who he was, hesitantly replied that he was the ex-husband of the bar owner; the female who was in the bar the previous day. He further explained that he had told security that he needed to speak with the investigator.

Establishing a rapport with the claimant's estranged husband, the witness volunteered that if his wife knew that he was talking with me, she would most likely take revenge against him in a drastic way.

He then nervously volunteered that his wife had lied to the insurance company when she signed the Statement of Loss and, that unknown to anyone but himself, she always kept two separate financial records and that the false and inflated income statement was going to be given to the insurance company in support of the recent renovations, past income and projected future income loss. He also told me that he had taken the original financial record book shortly before the fire and that he would give me those records if I promised to keep his name confidential.

In addition, he suggested that someone should talk to the chambermaid who had been paid by his ex-wife to start the fire. After obtaining his full name and where I could locate him for future communication, he quickly left the building.

Several hours later while I was still working in the building the ex-husband returned and handed me a plastic shopping bag which he said held the authentic financial records for the business. I quickly scanned the books, gave him a hand-written receipt and he again departed the building.

Armed with the incriminating evidence, I signed out of the fire scene and called an acquaintance that I knew to be well connected in the East Indian community. He was honest, forthcoming and had proven to be a reliable source of information in the past.

Upon arriving at his door and advising him of some the details of the investigation, he invited me into his home. Within minutes we were sitting in his living room and I began taking notes. The first thing the informant told me was the name of the chambermaid who was in fact a youthful 29-year-old married to an 80-year-old East Indian male. He explained the cultural aspects of the arranged marriage, and said that the elderly husband, who he knew quite well, told him that he was angry with his much younger wife for having had an affair and bringing disgrace into the family home. The contact provided me the name and address of the chambermaid's husband. Thanking him for the evidence, I departed his residence.

Arriving at the address provided by the informant, I was greeted by the elderly husband of the suspect; whereby he told me that his wife had raced home the afternoon of the pub fire smelling of smoke and gasoline and, that he personally observed his wife strip off her clothing, get into the shower and, after showering, place the soiled clothes in a sealed plastic bag. He reluctantly added that he watched her take the bag to the garbage can on the street.

According to the witness the refuse truck picked up the garbage within two hours of depositing the bag at the curb. It was incredible evidence and the disgruntled and ashamed octogenarian further told me that the pub owner, who was his wife's boss, had paid his wife to start the fire and directed her to get rid of any evidence in that regard.

Furthermore, the angry husband told me that his wife's employer had previously owned a motel in a city north of where we were and, that his wife's boss had also burned down that motel approximately ten years earlier and that the fire department had found a female chambermaid burned to death in one of the motel rooms at that location.

Within forty-five minutes of meeting the elderly male and having obtained a written statement, I drove approximately fifty kilometers north and located the motel referred to in the statement. Parking in front of the motel office, I noticed a middle-aged East Indian female behind the desk and, walking into the office took the direct approach and laid out exactly who I was and what was required of the front desk clerk. She advised me that she was the office manager and had been at the motel for many years.

To my absolute amazement, the office manager knew what I was referring to and confirmed that she recalled the fire at the motel ten years earlier and that a female employee had been burned to death in one of the motel rooms. The witness named the previous owner as being the subject of my current investigation.

After about an hour in the office speaking with the office manager, she provided a written statement whereby she detailed that she had been working the day of the fire, knew about the conspiracy to defraud the insurance company and, had been threatened by the subject of my investigation to keep quiet. It was unfathomable that the contact, who was lamenting the entire sordid story about the fire, conspiracy and resultant death of the chambermaid; had calculatingly covered up the previous fire, criminal negligence causing death and conspiracy to commit insurance fraud.

The witness was advised that she would be hearing from the police and that she was to detail to the police that I had obtained a written statement. This was done so that the police would know that I was not obstructing justice as there is no statute of limitations regarding homicide or negligent death.

After obtaining the statement, I departed the motel and drove back to the fire scene that had prompted the last two witness statements. However; I was unable to locate the pub owner or her estranged husband.

Feeling frustrated by the disappearance of the claimant and her estranged husband, I called my client and brought him up to date on the investigation and advised him that I was going to visit the local police detachment. After speaking with the client, I drove to the local police detachment and provided a copy of the three witness statements detailing the current arson, insurance fraud and the cover up of the previous fire and resultant death of the chambermaid ten years earlier.

Approximately two days later, while in the process of preparing an evidence package for my client, I learned from the first witness that I had spoken with at the beginning of the investigation, that the estranged husband had been found dead in a local ditch and that a hypodermic needle had been found stuck in his arm.

Calling the confidential informant, he advised me that the chambermaid who started the fire recently told her husband that the claimant had fled the country the night before and was hiding in a village in the Punjab region of India. He provided the name and address of where the claimant and now murder suspect was presently residing in India.

Through the assistance of the local RCMP detachment, I was able to speak with a corporal employed with Immigration & Extradition Canada and provided him the information about the suspect and her current address in India.

The following day the corporal phoned me and said that he and his partner had obtained an Extradition Order, were flying out of Vancouver International Airport later that evening and would be arresting the subject and returning her to Canada to answer for the ten year old arson file, murder of the chambermaid and the recent suspicious death of her estranged husband. I thanked the corporal for his report, as he did not have to call me and provide any details of the police file. His call indicated that the RCMP was grateful for my assistance.

In addition, I learned later from the local detachment that the chambermaid in the current investigation was charged with conspiracy to commit arson for financial remuneration. Based on that information, I concluded that the claimant had motive, opportunity and an eyewitness link to the fire. In addition, she was now a prime suspect in the death of her estranged husband and the death of the chambermaid 10 years earlier.

It was a difficult file and I am grateful for the cooperation of the fire department, police and confidential informant who provided information that resulted in the apprehension and conviction of the guilty persons: a clear indication of Guilty Knowledge.

The Latin phrase: *habeas corpus* means "the writ requiring a person under arrest to be brought before a judge or into court" and not necessarily requiring a dead body. The Latin phrase: *corpus delicti* means "basic elements of the crime, or the body of the evidence" and often gets confused with the concept that if there is no physical body then there is no *corpus deliciti.*

CHAPTER 12

Fire Investigation #2

This historic fire scene took place in a heritage home approximately 85 to 90 years old in a large ocean front mansion on Vancouver Island. The details of the case were that two professional men jointly owned and resided in a large six-bedroom home that was insured for several million dollars and designated a heritage building for the purpose of the preservation of historical buildings.

The details of the case were that a fire occurred in the 12-foot-high ceiling of the bottom floor, in the large room facing towards the ocean. The house was huge and approximately seven thousand square feet with stone work, Tudor style decor and a copper roof. There were also fireplaces downstairs and in every bedroom. The main ballroom was situated in the front east side of the building and displayed a wall to wall stone fronted fireplace.

The insurance adjustor told me that the fire department had responded rather quickly and extinguished the fire which had progressed downward, flashed up, rolled over on the ceiling and burned down onto the main floor causing significant structural damage to the main floor and basement below. The fire department reported to the insurance company that the cause of the fire was *undetermined* and that while overhauling the inferno; significant fire suppression and water damage had resulted.

My client asked if I would be willing to do a background investigation on the two professional men to determine if there was a financial motive to light the fire as a result of their lifestyles. It was a simple assignment and I immediately commenced a background check on both of the homeowners.

What most insurance claimants do not know, is that once a proof of claim form has been submitted, the claimant, or in this case the claimants, have virtually authorized the insurance company to conduct enquiries relative to financial history, claims history and a character background of the policy holders making a claim.

To assist in those inquiries, there is an organization called the Insurance Crime Prevention Bureau (ICPB) which maintains a complex and far reaching history of all suspicious claim applications in Canada and, the ICPB has the authority to research claim history and deny a claim for fraudulent reasons.

The discouraging factor about the ICPB is that the information is strictly confidential and generally not released to any third parties; unless criminal charges are preferred against the claimant.

Finding no indication of any impropriety or, conversely, motive for starting the fire for financial gain or personal animus, it was suggested to the client that I attend at the fire scene and commence a more thorough investigation. It was agreed and an investigation was now underway on the residence.

Generally, it is wise to conduct a walk-through of the fire scene before conferring with the local responding fire department. Entering the premises through the front double wide doors off a large covered porch with beams and pillars on both of the stairs, and going into the main entrance, I observed that there had in fact been significant fire suppression damage to the bottom floor in an attempt to save the beautiful heritage building.

The large windows were blown out on the main floor, which indicated a high degree of temperature in the room indicative of a flashover (pyrolysis – secondary ignition whereby heated gases generally ignite combustible materials in a low or high burning situation) whereby flames sought combustible material in the ceiling and, having little oxygen to feed the flames, rolled over causing a downward flashover effect. Based on that observation, it was apparent that the fire started in the ceiling beneath the second floor.

Going upstairs and inspecting the floor in the upstairs hallway, I observed blistering, paint scorching and evidence of soot and smoke damage to the floor of a large bathroom. Using a fire axe, I chopped out a portion of the floor and noticed that the sub floor was encased in a lath and plaster hollow space. Knowing that homes built during the turn of the century used plaster and lath strips to encase ceilings, I took some pictures and left the fire scene.

Returning to our office, I commenced a Google search of fire history in ceilings of heritage homes and found an article written by a fire chief in Chicago by the surname of Anderson. It was an interesting article and referred to a theory, put forward by Fire Chief Anderson stating that in turn of the century homes; lead pipes were often sealed in ceilings that were encased in lath and plaster to hide the pipes.

Chief Anderson's article further revealed that lead hot water pipes sealed in floors and ceilings more than seventy-five years ago created an ambient temperature build up over time that was capable of self-igniting combustible materials: usually cedar lath and bursting into flames which eventually burned down and onto the floor below. To further confuse the scientology of the low burning phenomenon, the burning material on the floor below created a secondary point of ignition that progressed into a flashover after reaching the ceiling above from the process of pyrolysis (heated gases igniting within the heat temperature) which quickly engulfed the entire room, masking the condition of pyrophoric burning (heat transfer of ambient and trapped air).

This phenomenon was aptly named: *"Anderson's Theory of Pyrophoric Burning"*, and being fascinated by this incredible bit of knowledge, I located Chief Anderson in Chicago, Illinois and discussed his theory in relation to the ceiling fire that I was investigating in the heritage home in Canada. He immediately agreed with the determination of subject fire. It was an amazing determination and the insurance client paid out the claim and the theory became history in British Columbia. My colleague at the local fire department happened to be named Anderson as well and was excited to bring this new theory to the attention of the Canadian Association of Fire Investigators.

CHAPTER 13

Natural Gas Explosion Case #1

The investigation of natural or man caused explosions tends to be one of the most demanding tasks of gathering evidence in support of determination or cause. Homicide investigations are, of course, the number one offense requiring an immediate gathering of facts: as the first 48 hours are crucial to the success of the investigation and, ultimate conviction. However; not all criminal acts or acts of negligence are afforded the opportunity of time. The following case clearly points out that fact and, is about a natural gas explosion causing death that was initially investigated in a negligent manner nearly a year after the incident.

This case came to my attention approximately eleven months after the explosion, death and total destruction of a residence in a medium sized city on Vancouver Island, British Columbia.

An insurance client hired me to investigate the events leading up to the cause of a natural gas explosion, whereby a gas furnace in the basement of a large single family dwelling, situated on the corner of two intersecting streets, suddenly blew up and completely destroyed the home and killed the male occupant in the house at the time of the explosion. The date of loss was noted as October 27th.

The reports provided from the client were significant in detail and extremely subjective in nature. The extensive post explosion report had been prepared by the gas company who had initially constructed the gas line which was eventually connected to the residence in question. Unfortunately for my client, the extensive and obviously expensive report was greatly biased in favour of the large and prosperous gas company.

Making detailed notes from the information provided, it was immediately apparent that not all the information in the report was conclusive and appeared to be subjective in nature. In fact, it appeared to be more contrived than factual; something that a layperson would not thoroughly comprehend. In fact, the report was provided as more of a *red herring* than a determination of cause.

Attending the scene, it was noted that the only evidence remaining of the house was a levelled foundation and perimeter landscape, inclusive of bark mulch and a plastic ground barrier partially buried under the garden mulch. Obtaining photographs of the foundation, perimeter and landscape items, I commenced a canvass of the neighbourhood in anticipation of obtaining information about the explosion. Canvassing a scene nearly a year later rarely provides sustainable leads or results; however, it is an important step in a fire or gas explosion determination of cause.

The first two residences visited in the immediate area of the explosion did not provide any related information, as the occupants had been at work that fatal day. Moving a bit further from the scene, I attended at a residence across the road and north of the explosion site and had the opportunity to interview an elderly female who stated that she had lived in her home for many years prior to the incident. The contact immediately invited me into her home and commenced a long litany of events leading up to the explosion and resultant investigation by the gas company. The witness was amazing in her recollection of facts considering her age and duration of time since the explosion; however, the 90 something witness unknowingly provided a source of information that provided a direct relationship to the cause of the explosion.

The witness volunteered that about three or four weeks prior to the explosion and, more recently, two days before the explosion, she had called the municipal office responsible for public works and gas line regulations at around 11 o'clock p.m. and left a message on the answering machine complaining that there was a strong odour of a rotten egg smell in the area. She recalled that her complaints should have been logged with the appropriate office but that no one responded to her concerns. In addition, the elderly witness informed me that she had never been questioned by anyone before or after the explosion; and simply did not make the connection between her phone call to public works or, conversely, speaking with any other authorities *after* the house on the corner blew up and the male owner was killed.

Natural gas in the purest of states is odourless, tasteless and colourless. Because of that state, a harmless chemical called Mercaptan is added to natural gas to alert individuals and/or professionals to the sour smelling odour in the event of a gas leak. Many people describe the odour of this additive as similar to rotten eggs. The elderly witness's statement about the rotten egg smell was extremely relevant and led me to check the area for any other sources of natural gas usage.

Standing on the crossroad of the main street in front of the victim's previous home and, looking at the side street on the north side of the destroyed residence, I noticed an elementary school directly up from and opposite the seat of the explosion.

Attending at the school and obtaining permission to speak with the maintenance person responsible for the heating system in the building, I learned that the school was heated by natural gas and that the gas line was in fact situated on the south side of the road (directly adjacent to the explosion) and that the maintenance person had in fact brought to the attention of the gas company - pre explosion, about a small gas leak in one of the gas lines connected to the school. Our witness stated that the gas leak was repaired and there had been no direct connection of that previous gas leak to the subsequent explosion across the street. In fact, the witness was clear that the leak had been repaired months before the explosion on the corner.

Leaving the community school, I attended at the local municipal office and spoke with the engineer responsible for public works and natural gas line connections on behalf of the natural gas company. Looking back in the logs, the engineer was able to advise that there had been a call from the school of a gas leak on their property and, that the gas line had in fact been repaired at that location and no other reports received.

Confirming that information, I further questioned the engineer if there had been any complaints about a rotten egg smell prior to the explosion and the engineer checked the municipal register and located a message that had been left on the nightshift answering machine; which unfortunately had been discredited as someone complaining about a rotten egg smell that was most likely related to the local pulp mill odour, which quite often permeated the city and surrounding area. This was a major breakthrough in the investigation and I determined, from that disclosure, there had been more than just a simple gas leak near or at the school prior to the explosion.

Returning to the scene of the explosion, I commenced an examination of the perimeter of the property and discovered that the bark mulch surrounding the rear area of the house was covering a large blue tarp; which extended around the rear and north side of the former house perimeter. Digging down, I found a small trench which appeared to have been caused by the ingress of a liquid.

Taking photographs, and suspecting that the natural gas leak had leeched down under the side street in front of the school, gone under the bark mulch and settled on top of the vapour barrier (tarp) and, over a period of time had leeched under the foundation of the existing house and settled near the gas furnace (substantiated by the house blueprints) which had been located at the exact same corner of the basement in relationship to the leeching of the natural gas.

The most common of the chemical explosions are those caused by the burning of combustible hydrocarbon fuels. These are combustion explosions and are characterized by the presence of a fuel with air as an oxidizer and may also involve dusts. Combustion reactions are classified as either detonations or deflagrations: depending on the velocity of the flame from propagation through the fuel.

Detonations and deflagrations are two ways which energy may be released - if the explosion moves outwards at supersonic speeds (faster than the speed of sound at 1100 feet per second), it is a detonation, while the action of deflagration is to push the air in front and move at a slower rate than a detonation. There is also an audible difference between the two; however, most people can't tell the difference as the explosion occurs at supersonic speed. The evidence of either one is significant to a fire/explosion investigator.

Fuel gases that escape from their piping, storage, or utilization systems can serve as easily ignited fuels for fires and explosions. The open flames of fuel gas burners or pilot lights can also serve as competent ignition sources for fuel gases and other fuels; particularly flammable gases or the vapours of ignitable liquids and dusts. Ignition temperatures for most fuel gases range from 723 degrees Fahrenheit to approximately 1170 degrees Fahrenheit.

Looking again at the origin of the explosion, I was able to determine that the point of ignition and subsequent explosion did in fact occur near the placement of the furnace. This was determined to be a *blast pressure wave effect gas* explosion.

High order damage would show shattered and splintered remains of a four-bedroom home. The effects of the explosion of a material produce a large quantity of gases. These gases expand at a high rate of speed and move outward from the point of origin. The gases and the displaced air moved by those gases produce a pressure front that is primarily responsible for the damage, injuries and/or deaths associated with the explosion.

In the case of this particular explosion, it was evident that someone had cleared up the debris and that the remains of the foundation indicated a high-order damage explosion. Effects of explosions can be observed in four major groups: blast pressure wave effect, shrapnel effect, thermal effect, and seismic effect.

My resultant determination was that natural gas had pooled under the foundation in a confined space (between the vapour barrier, perimeter vapour barrier tarp and bark mulch placed around the foundation) and, when the victim re-lit the furnace in the early fall, the pooled gas ignited in the confined space causing an explosion.

Upon submitting my report, it was my understanding that the insurance client subrogated the claim expenses against the gas company and the municipality; as it had conclusively been determined that the gas leak at the school had in fact caused a series of events that precipitated an explosion, destroyed the home and killed the occupant.

CHAPTER 14

Accelerant Fire Case #1

In the early spring of 2002, I received a call from an insurance adjuster in Victoria who was concerned about a structure fire, causing significant damage to a residence in Tofino on Vancouver Island. As the distance to the fire scene was approximately 187 kilometers, I gathered my fire investigations kit: complete with axe, mask, rubber gloves, charts, measuring tapes, electrical equipment, notebooks, cameras and coveralls and headed off in a direction north west of Port Alberni. The drive took an entire day and by the time I arrived at the destination, I secured a motel for a minimum of two days.

On the first day of the investigation, having alerted the local fire commissioner (Fire Chief) and the homeowner that I would be on their property for several days, I attended at the two-story open carport, single family dwelling on a treed area on the southeast side of the street.

Walking onto the property, I conducted a perimeter search of the exterior of the property and adjacent properties and commenced taking photographs of the yard and building. As stated previously, the theory in fire investigations is to start with the least fire damage and progress to the most extensive fire or structural damage to determine a point of origin; allowing of course, that the building or structure is still intact.

In this particular case, the fire progressed up the carport stairs, entered the second story kitchen door and progressed through the house. After obtaining a series of progressive photographs and a video of the house and property, I went back to the street, which was approximately forty-five feet from the open carport and observed that a large propane tank sat under the open concrete carport, to the right of the floor, directly in line and below the second-floor kitchen door and under a plywood ceiling of the open carport. Above the carport appeared to be a second story room south of the kitchen, with a deck on the outside of that room. Attending in the carport, I observed soot on the left side of the propane tank and charred steps leading up to the charred and burned doorway on the second floor, which was nailed shut with a piece of angled plywood.

Conducting a thorough examination of the propane tank to establish volume, manufacturer, Canada Safety Codes and year of production, I observed that the gas flow copper line that connects to the tank regulator and was intended to go into the house at the west side of the carport wall, was missing. In addition, I noticed that about 8 inches of a charred neoprene rubber type hose was still connected to the regulator valve. This was a major revelation, as natural and propane gas tanks are required by manufacturing regulations to be fitted with CSA approved copper gas lines.

Taking numerous photographs of the carport, propane tank and adjacent wall, I proceeded up the charred entryway stairs, removed the plywood brace from in front of the door and entered the house.

Upon stepping into the heavily fire and smoke damaged kitchen, adjacent dining room and living room located on the northeast front side of the house, I observed low burning patterns indicative of oxygen fanning whereby a wind or gust of air enhanced rapid movement of oxygen carrying the fire load in the direction of combustible materials. A perfect example of oxygen fed fire load. The burn patterns progressing up the walls and towards the ceiling were located on the west side of the upstairs door and moved away from the corner wall where the propane tank was situated on the carport below. After taking notes and obtaining photographs, I returned to the carport, boarded the doorway and commenced canvassing the immediate neighbourhood, directing myself directly across the street where a neighbouring house faced the carport of the claimant's home.

It only took a few minutes to learn from the neighbour that the fire under the carport started around 3:35 p.m. at which time the occupant's teenage son arrived home from school and, upon entering the open carport went into the utility shed at the rear of the carport and was observed carrying a large rectangular cardboard box from the shed which the teenager laid down on the carport and proceeded to tear the box into several smaller pieces.

According to the witness, who observed the actions of the teenage male from their front window across the street, the teenage male piled the cardboard in the driveway, directly in front of the propane tank and lit the cardboard in an attempt to burn the large box to avoid having to take the box to the recycle depot. The witness described the box as approximately eight to ten feet long, about six inches deep and four feet high. Something like a box used to hold a standard door or large frame of some sort.

At the same time that the teenager lit the cardboard box, a gust of wind blew into the driveway, fanned the burning cardboard increasing the height of the flames and scattered the burning box pieces into the carport and onto the propane tank. Fueled by a fresh source of oxygen, the ignited cardboard box landed on the propane tank and began charring the outside of the tank where the neoprene gas line was attached. Panicking, the teenage boy raced up the stairs, opened the kitchen door and attempted to find a bucket to fill with water in an effort to douse the now roaring fire.

Unfortunately, the fire progressed rapidly and fearing that the fire was getting out of control, the boy raced down the stairs and went next door to call the fire department. By the time the fire department arrived, the stairs, upper kitchen, dining room and living room were totally engulfed. What was interesting was that no one from the local fire department questioned the neighbour across the street and, no determination was made as to the point of origin of the fire. This utterly amazed me, as it was obvious that the propane gas fuel line was missing from the propane tank.

After interviewing the teenage boy later that afternoon, with the consent of his parents, he reluctantly confessed that he had been burning a large cardboard box in front of the carport and, thinking that he was in control of the burn, was shocked when a gust of wind, obviously more than a sudden gust, blew the burning cardboard into the carport and landed it against the propane tank and on the outside stairs ascending to the second floor.

The sequence of events determined by

this investigation established that the burning cardboard blew up against the regulator valve of the propane tank and that the flames ignited the neoprene fuel line, burning the line from a point between the middle of the tank and the carport wall: thereby causing a whipsaw action of the partially burned hose which then spewed pressurized gas propelled flames against the west side of the house exterior wall, raced up the wooden stairs through the open door and progressed throughout the house, effectively blow torching the residence.

Had the kitchen door been closed, the fire would have been contained to the open carport and the bottom of the stairs. Unfortunately, with the second story door open, a new oxygen source became available and the fire raced up the stairs and into the house. To further establish that theory, the upstairs patio door exiting from the kitchen was in fact open at the time of the fire. It was a perfect wind tunnel and a new source of oxygen.

In speaking with the fire department earlier, I learned that from the time they received the 911 call, the volunteer fire department responded to the residence within sixteen minutes, thereby giving the fire a good start on the interior of the home. By the time the fire department attended at the residence, the propane tank was empty and fire suppression concentrated on the interior of the house. It was indeed a confusing point of origin as no one made a determination about the cause of the fire as there was no combustible material on or near the propane tank. In fact, I learned that the fire department failed to determine that the propane tank gas line was missing and assumed that the copper gas line had been removed *after* the fire had been supressed. Another theory was that the propane tank had been empty and not in use at the time of the fire, a misdirected assumption that necessitated a fire causation investigation on the part of the insurance company.

In my report to the insurance company, it was detailed that the rubber neoprene hose attached to the propane tank regulator was not to code and had melted during the initial commencement of burning from the cardboard, thereby creating a secondary source of fuel and resultant damage to the carport, stairs and upper rooms of the residence. As the claim was paid to the insured, it was not necessary to testify in that investigation.

CHAPTER 15

Fire Investigation #3

The suspicious fire and total destruction of a large commercial retail business on the secondary street of a 50,000 plus population city on Vancouver Island generated considerable attention.

The 10,000 plus square foot building was situated on the edge of a large shopping mall, parallel to the main roadway exiting off the Trans-Canada Highway within two blocks of the downtown city core. The mall was leased to local merchants from the First Nations band office and considerable controversy had been present several months prior to the fire as a result of the landlord wanting to increase the lease payments from the mall tenants.

Several of the large stores had considered terminating their lease and moving to another mall north of the city presently being constructed. However; the fire at the large commercial building was not part of that controversy and they had no intention of moving their business elsewhere.

On a cool October morning, the local commercial auto parts building was completely destroyed by fire before the local fire department could supress the raging inferno. The building was stocked with rubber tires, fuel-based petroleum products and numerous other combustible materials. Gallantly though they tried, the local fire department, well known for rapid response and the adjoining community's mutual aid were not successful in getting the fire out before the interior of the building was structurally damaged beyond repair. The damage to the building was a large financial hit to the business owners and the community as the store was the only major auto parts distributor within 50 kilometers. Fire investigators were able to determine the cause of the fire as arson; however, no suspects were identified and the loss of the building, merchant's inventory and business interruption was catastrophic. The determination was that the building exterior had been doused with an accelerant and ignited.

Not being part of the initial investigative team, I was hired by the insurance company to try and locate any witnesses within the community. As is expected, rumours abound and the community had all manner of delinquent characters in mind; however, nothing came of those rumours.

Being provided with the details of the fire investigation, I concurred with the cause of the fire: which determined that a large amount of petroleum accelerant had been doused all around the rear perimeter of the building and ignited gas containers thrown through the broken exterior windows. Based on the flow of traffic being greatly diminished after 11:00 p.m. the fire was deemed to have been ignited after 2:00 am, which was supported by the call to 911 which came in around 2:34 a.m. - a considerable amount of time for total involvement of the fire.

Months later, while still keeping the assignment on the back burner (no pun intended), and while working numerous other cases on the island, I happened to take an early afternoon coffee break at a local pub near the vicinity of the fire. Incidentally, the pub had also been destroyed by arson twenty years earlier.

Sitting in a far corner of the pub, drinking a coffee and reading my investigators notebook relative to the current case that I was investigating, a female unknown to me approached my table and asked if I was the fire investigator looking for information on the recent commercial fire around the corner. Inviting the lady to sit for a moment and, acknowledging who I was, the contact revealed that she knew who had caused the fire and the reason for their actions. Not surprisingly, this happens to me quite often during the course of investigations - so I invited the source of new information to speak freely after suggesting that I might be able to protect her identity.

The confidential witness told me that two teenage Aboriginal boys, whom she knew from community contact, set the fire in the middle of a dark, overcast night, believing that the fire would force the tenants to vacate the lease. This was an interesting concept and when I enquired of the names of the two boys, she advised me that she had spoken to no one for fear of retaliation. Learning of this fact, I advised her that I was required to provide the information to the local authorities and, that she would definitely be questioned by the police.

Learning the suspects' names and not being able to assure anonymity, I departed the pub with information that would indeed create considerable friction within the community. Believing that I could speak with the Elders of the tribe, I proceed to the local band office and spoke with a respected member of the tribal band council. After explaining that I was mandated to report the names to the police and my client, the Elder agreed to proceed and we made the call.

Fortunately, very little was said in the community as the boys were not adults and their names were protected by the *Youth Criminal*

Justice Act (in the Criminal Justice System) which applies to youth between the ages of 12 to 17. However, to the relief of the building owners, the insurance company had already built a new store as arson is not a legal reason for denying a fire insurance claim. In summary, very few people in the community knew of my investigation and subsequent results, as the names of the perpetrators was not disclosed. In addition, I do not know what measures the Elders took in administering Aboriginal justice to the delinquent youth.

CHAPTER 16

Civil Investigation Case #2

A well-known and highly respected criminal defence lawyer called my office and asked if I could attend with him at his place of business and open a new file. No indication was offered about the file and the lawyer advised that we would be meeting with his client at that time.

Attending the next day with the lawyer and his client, I was hired to gather information about the names and former addresses of any of the previous staff at the Port Alberni Residential School; to advance sexual abuse claims against the school educators. To my relief, the client had a variation of most of the names which might prove reliable. In addition, I was hired to locate a possible witness who had been a naval reservist out of Esquimalt B.C. and had worked during the summer at the school approximately 30 years earlier.

In that regard, I was given the last name of the naval reservist whose last name sounded something like "snow", and the fact that he had been a marine engineer. To my frustration, very little information could be provided as the abuse had taken place in the late fifties and sixties and the police had not been able to solicit much support from the community. However; I was provided the name of the senior ranking police officer who had been working on the file several years before. Unfortunately, the police were unable to provide much background and I was left to my own resources.

The Indian Residential School System was created by the Dominion Government of Canada in the mid-1880's and operated until the last school was shut down in 1973. There were various residential schools in British Columbia and tremendous psychological trauma and physical harm was perpetrated upon our innocent First Nations students.

Determined to conclude the case, I proceeded to the village of Port Alberni and began the difficult task of looking for witnesses. It was daunting work and feeling frustrated I walked over to the park and sat on a bench overlooking the Alberni Canal and, while looking at the ocean in front of me; began praying for an answer.

After about 15 minutes I remembered an investigative tool that I had learned while trying to locate people for document service. One of my colleagues had taught me that old phone books were an exceptional source of information, as phone books back in the fifties and sixties printed people's names, occupations and place of employment - a good start to any investigation.

Setting off to find the local museum, I came across a little old building by the railway tracks. Going into the museum with renewed vigor, I had the pleasure of meeting an octogenarian volunteer who told me that she was 86 years old and had been a "two day a week" volunteer at the museum for over 40 years.

Her name was Anne, and she loved to chat about her community. Feeling instant trust in this delightful local pioneer, I willingly produced my credentials, told her I was an investigator and the purpose of my enquiries. With a glint in her captivating and immensely wise eyes, Ms. Anne starting talking about the attic and "old and musty papers" that might help with the enquiries. On a roll, I asked her if she knew of any old phone books dating back 40 or 50 years. Looking at the clock, Ms. Anne told me that she had to close the museum in about ten minutes and that there was not enough time to make my way up to the attic and that she would not be back to the museum until the following Wednesday, as she only volunteered two days a week. I recall expressing my disappointment as it was Wednesday and Ms. Anne would not be back again until the following week. My concern was that she would forget who I was and that I would lose the opportunity to obtain possession of the old phone books. Not to be discouraged, I promised to phone Ms. Anne the following Tuesday afternoon and remind her that I would be returning to Port Alberni the following day. Ms. Anne gave me a museum card and promised to help me the following week.

With dreaded concern, I drove the 167 kilometers back home and became immersed in my ongoing case load. As a point of interest, I am often referred to as a "dog with a bone" once I get a sniff of a clue or an idea about obtaining information or facts and, it is really frustrating for me to wait on future leads.

The following Tuesday morning I called the museum and eventually got through to the delightful Ms. Anne. At first, she was confused as to who I was; however, when I mentioned that I was the private investigator looking for old phone books, she was audibly brightened and said that she would get one of the younger lads, who happened to be in the building for a few hours, to get up to the attic and bring down the old phone books. I was enthralled and told my new friend Ms. Anne that I would see her early the following morning.

At around o-dark-hundred on a

Wednesday morning during an overcast October day, I gathered my files and headed for Port Alberni, arriving at the museum at around 9:30 a.m. To my dismay, the door was locked and a sign on the door indicated that the museum was closed until 11:00 a.m. due to volunteer illness. I was devastated and decided to go across the street and wait for the museum to open. Sure enough, at around ten minutes to eleven, a middle-aged male opened the door of the museum. Trotting across the road, I went inside and asked the male if Ms. Anne would be in today. With a pure look of pain, the volunteer told me that Ms. Anne was ill and had been unable to open the museum at 9:30 a.m. that morning. Not being dissuaded, I asked if he had been the person who had brought the phone books down from the attic the previous day. Seeing a confused look on his face, my hopes began to fade. However, thinking on my feet, I asked him if I could look around for the boxes of phone books and reluctantly he agreed. Within minutes, I located three dusty old cardboard boxes behind a table over by the sign-in desk. With trembling fingers, I turned back the tops and, to my absolute joy, found the dusty and musty phone books.

Exclaiming my elation, I asked the volunteer if I could take the boxes over to a quiet corner of the museum and spend the day going through the books. My second disappointment of the day was when he lamented that he had to close the museum early that day as he had another appointment in town. I began to negotiate for time and eventually earned and extra two and a half hours. Looking at the clock above the door, I knew that two and a half hours would be a tight timeline to find the information that I so desperately needed. Emptying all three boxes, I organized them by year and started scanning the pages looking for anyone who had been employed at the Residential School.

To my benefit, there were only about nine phone books during the relevant time frame that I needed to locate the school staff. With only minutes to spare, I found the last name I had been looking for which provided me with a list of the full name, middle initial, occupation, address and phone number: school teacher, administrator and clerical staff. I was overjoyed and compiled a list of 11 educators and the school administrator.

Needing to photocopy the relevant pages in the books created a wee bit of stress to the patient male at the counter and, after lamenting the fact that I had driven for over four hours to get to the museum, the volunteer relented and helped me photocopy the pages that I had placed book marks in over the duration of my transcribing the information. Within 15 minutes after the volunteer wanted to leave, I departed with the coveted prize. It was indeed a gold mine of information.

Having obtained the names and former addresses of the school teachers and the administrator, I decided to stay the night in an attempt to locate their former houses before retiring for the evening. By 7:45 p.m. that evening, in a miserable rain storm, I located all the former houses that were on my list and decided to make an effort to knock on the doors of those homes in the morning to see if anyone knew of the people on my list.

The following morning my excitement was hard to contain and by noon that day I had spoken to most of the homeowners at the addresses on my list. Of the 12 names, seven were remembered as leaving the area when the school closed in 1973. Of the educators, I was able to learn where they had family or had moved to when the school closed. It was invigorating and I continued my search for the remainder of the suspects. By two o'clock that day I had compiled a list of the other suspects and learned that one had moved to Australia, another was in Ontario, and the rest were still in British Columbia and that the school administrator had moved to the lower mainland outside of Vancouver, B.C. In addition, I learned later that the School Priest Arthur Henry Plint had been charged, convicted and sentenced to 11 years in prison and that the School Principal John Andrew's had been called as a witness at that trial and denied knowing about the sexual abuse. Returning back to my office that evening, I created a wall board and placed the suspect's names on the board to coincide with their tenure at the school. After compiling a list of names, I finished for the day.

The next challenge was to locate the witness whose major clue to me was that his last name sounded like "snow". Not being daunted and being retired Navy; I called a contact in National Defence Headquarters in Ottawa and enquired if his department still had the microfiche films that the navy used in the 50's and 60's to register naval reservists who served during that period of time. I further knew that the witness had been a marine engineer (engine room stoker) and was about 19 years of age in 1969. Leaving the information with my contact, I put the file in my "in basket" and, to my absolute shock, received a telephone call two days later identifying the naval reservist by full name, address and current phone number.

It was amazing information and at approximately 7:48 p.m. that evening, while concluding a surveillance job in Victoria, I called the witness at his residence. The call to the witness went something like this:

"Good evening sir, I am looking for Mr. ……."

The answer which caused a tingling

down my spine came as:

"Yes, I am he - who is calling?"

With more than obvious excitement in my voice, I identified who I was and the purpose for my call. The response was absolutely not expected when the witness replied:

"I have been waiting over thirty years for this phone call. When can we meet?"

The following day, the lawyer client and I attended with the witness at his home and obtained a sworn statement regarding his recollection of being a witness to the abuse at the school. As a point of interest, the reason that the witness was not required to disclose the abuse was by virtue of the fact that he was not legally bound by a *statutory obligation* to disclose abuse of children. However, I question the morality of that legality, whereby non-professionals who worked in schools during that period of time, were not mandated to disclose sexual abuse of children. I also believe that everyone who is aware of such abuse should be held to the same standard; however, in defence of the witness, a then 19 year old reserve sailor employed to work as a temporary janitor at the school, had observed the abuse while he was looking for something in a broom closet and had been frightened to reveal himself.

Coming close to solving a case that had been on the books for over thirty years, I became resolved to find the eleven educators and the school administrator and provide their names and addresses to the client and hopefully the police.

Over the next few weeks, I was able to locate nine of the eleven former educators and, to my absolute joy learned later that there were several convictions coming out of the civil law suit against the Federal Department of Indian Affairs and the United Church of Canada. Justice Donald Brenner convened the hearing on June 4th, 1998 and the healing process commenced as numerous victims of Residential School Abuse were vindicated for their years of suffering. On August 2nd, 1973 the Tseshaht First Nations commemorated the closing of the Port Alberni Residential School and brought the children home.

The Port Alberni Residential Abuse Investigation was a case file that I will not forget and the fight for Truth and Reconciliation must never end if Canada is to truly rise as a world leader.

CHAPTER 17

Civil Investigation Case #3
The Cover-Up Murder of Johnny Sticks

About a year after working on the Port Alberni Residential School investigation, I received a telephone call from the administrator of the Alkali Lake Shuswap (Secwepemc) First Nations band office who asked for me by name.

During the initial introduction from the administrator, she told me that my name had been recommended by the Royal Canadian Mounted Police, Aboriginal Policing Organization resultant of my work on the Port Alberni Residential School Investigation. I was intrigued by the conversation and agreed to take on the case.

The administrator explained that an eight-year-old Residential School student by the name of Johnny Sticks had been found dead in a snowbank on the Alkali Reserve in the winter of 1908, and the generations of survivors of the late Johnny Sticks were looking for closure regarding his suspicious death.

Speculation had always run high in the First Nation's community over the death of Johnny Sticks and, the band council agreed to hire my services to investigate Johnny's death. Without hesitation, I agreed to take the case and eagerly awaited a facsimile from the band office providing the little known details of his demise

Unfortunately, very little information was available. Realizing that I was dealing with a 90-year-old suspicious death case, I pondered the next move, which led to my attending at the Vital Statics office in Victoria. Of course, no one there was remotely aware of the 1908 case and they directed me to the B.C. Provincial Archives.

Dressed in black shoes, a pair of slacks, cotton shirt and sports jacket, I signed into the Archives filled with apprehension resultant of the female gate-keeper at the front desk who very promptly and directly told me that no copies of any documents could be removed from the Archives without express approval of the archivist: who happened to be away on vacation for a month.

Agreeing to all of the imposed conditions of the adamant gate-keeper, I made my way to the microfiche section of the large building. The B.C. Archives Library is situated on the corner of Simcoe and Government Streets adjacent to the Parliament Buildings where I had been previously employed in late 1989 and early 1990 as a Ministerial Assistant to a former Provincial Cabinet Minister during the Vanderzalm Social Credit government.

Not familiar with the microfiche system in the museum, I asked a female working on one of the machines where I could locate historical coroner reports and was directed to a shelf stacked with round metal canisters standing upright on a wooden shelf.

Scanning the microfiche tins, I located a film canister dating between the years 1900 to 1910. Returning to the microfiche machine, I laboriously began searching for coroner reports from the beginning of the reel.

The task was tedious and, scrolling down the tapes was time consuming and caused considerable eye strain. However, several hours later I struck pay dirt. There in front of my weary eyes was the 1908 coroner's report for eight-year-old Johnny Sticks.

Before attending at the Archives, I had done some research on the history of the Dominion Government of Canada's *Coroner's Act*. Not knowing that I would be directed to the Archives, my research paid off by virtue of the fact that I had learned from my earlier research that the *Coroner's Act* drastically changed in 1921 to the effect that a coroner could no longer unilaterally rule on a suspicious death without the Crown appointing and constituting a Coroner's Inquest or Coroner's Court.

The coroner's report on Johnny sticks was an amazing find, as the report I was looking at was hand written with a quill pen and most likely an ink pot, and signed by the local coroner of the day: without the legal requirement to convene a Coroner's Inquest or Coroner's Court.

The laboriously written quill pen report recorded that eight-year-old Indian Residential School student Johnny Sticks had been beaten to death at the hand of the headmaster who had, without regard for human life, left his beaten body in a snow bank. The report further stated that "the Department of Indian and Northern Affairs had made a decision, in the best interest of the Residential School System, to cover up the brutal *death by beating* of Johnny Sticks" and had rationalized the murder in an attempt to promote the government Residential School agenda.

Not only was I angered and ashamed of our forefathers, but needed to devise a means to remove the dreadful cover-up report from the Archives. Thinking of a way to get past the gate-keeper, I devised a plan to remain seated at the microfiche machine until the last minute of the day so that my departure would be inconspicuous among the patrons leaving at the closure of the Archives.

While I was devising a way to innocuously print the one-page document, I noticed a smartly dressed female in a grey business suit seated at one of the other microfiche machines several chairs from where I was seated. Engaging in an inane conversation about the Archives, I asked the lady how I could print a one-page document.

Her response lifted my spirits as she told me to highlight the document, open a small window at the top right of the page, type the page number in the box and send the page to the printer, which was located behind our machines. Before I started the operation, the female, who I suspected to be a law student, told me that I needed a printer designation number.

Looking dismayed, I expostulated that I was from out of town and did not have a printer designation. Smiling from two seats away she volunteered her printer number and, with a flick of my finger, I sent the historical document to the printer. As I was getting up, I smiled at her and casually said: "Please don't interrupt your search; I can retrieve the one page myself." She smiled knowingly and I closed off the document, removed the microfiche spool and returned the canister to the shelf.

Within seconds I had the 14 ½ inch page in my hand. Now the next chore was to get the document out of the Archives: a task that I was beginning to feel guilty over. However, I immediately justified my actions considering the justice and closure that the document would eventually provide to the descendants of Johnny Sticks. Folding the one-page document three times from bottom to centre and from top to center, I slipped the highly coveted document into the left breast pocket of my sports jacket; telling myself that I was grateful for wearing the convenient jacket that particular day: a last minute decision before leaving home earlier that morning.

The resultant release of the document to the Alkali band office resounded around the country within weeks and, the Prime Minister of Canada made a special trip to the Secwepemc First Nation Reserve and presented a rather large cheque to the survivors of eight year old Johnny Sticks. This was the second time that I had been provided the opportunity to bring a semblance of justice and reconciliation to the First Nations People of British Columbia. It was indeed an honour.

CHAPTER 18

Criminal Case #5

During an extremely busy time with a heavy caseload, I received a telephone message from a female criminal defence lawyer in Victoria, British Columbia who stated that she had obtained authority from Legal Aid to hire my services in a homicide conviction appeal. The appellant was currently incarcerated in a federal institution and remonstrating to anyone that would listen that he was not guilty of murder but rather self-defence as a result of being in the wrong place at the wrong time.

Attending with the convicted man's lawyer and obtaining a court transcript of the jury trial and initial police investigation (disclosure documents), I started working on the file. The positive thing about capital case appeals is that the majority of the evidence has been reviewed, presented, released and available to the appeal team.

Spending the entire day reading over all the evidence, viewing photographs, perusing witness statements and going over the Crown's case, I was able to create a wall board of the time line and sequence of events leading up to the shooting of a known drug dealer in a mobile home park north of Victoria.

The difficulty of most appeal cases was locating and interviewing Crown and defence witnesses; particularly involving a case that took place some nine years earlier. However, like every file that we opened in our company since starting Ace in 1990, due diligence was something that we exercised with obsessive vigor as, at this time, I was to be the voice of the client.

Creating an investigative road map and making an appointment to interview the client (convicted male) in the federal prison was generally quite easy being a former Corrections Officer (post military) and, obtaining clearance from the institution required minimal paperwork. Upon attending at the prison and meeting with the appellant, I observed that he was a quiet, unassuming man of forty-six years of age who spoke with an east coast accent. As I only had about ninety minutes to learn about the client, I asked him where he came from in Nova Scotia. His demeanour changed noticeably and he mentioned a place in the Annapolis Valley that I knew well from my Military Basic Training Course (Boot Camp) at *HMCS Cornwallis*, Nova Scotia. As I shared how beautiful the valley was in spring, summer and fall, I sensed an immediate change in his attitude, a noticeable change in the client that would most likely create a more honest, forthright and personal communication between us, as we worked together for his freedom.

During this initial visit the client told me that he had been living in his older model travel trailer at the not-so-appealing campground for about ten months. His unit was parked in the trees on the west side of the overcrowded park.

The only positive factor about the location of his unit was the fact that his trailer was backed in near the bank of a small creek where he enjoyed sitting on the creek bank "spacing out" on nature. The downside was that the other RV's were in close proximity to his trailer and "everyone knew each other's business."

The client shared that he had been experiencing trouble with the male and his attractive blonde girlfriend in the campsite directly north of his unit and, that the man was a known drug dealer and prone to violent outbursts. Arguments, threats and a steady flow of drug dealing traffic came through the laneway night and day. In addition, the neighbour's girlfriend owned an expense white Dodge van, complete with chrome roof racks, tinted windows, inside curtains and all the additional aftermarket accessories. The client further remonstrated that the vehicle stood out from all the other *trailer park clunkers.* He expostulated that it was outstanding to everyone, including the park management who believed that the vehicle was used for transporting drugs and had been purchased from proceeds of crime. It was also a known fact, from conversations that my client had with the drug dealer's girlfriend, that the van was used to carry drugs across the Canadian border from the United States, and that during one such conversation, the blonde-haired neighbour told my client that she had rented a storage unit close by where she kept cash and drugs if she were ever required to flee in a hurry or, if her boyfriend became overly violent and the police were called. This information was a red flag as the drug dealer had exhibited an *out of control* rage at anyone who communicated with his beautiful and entrepreneurial girlfriend.

The convicted man explained that over a period of time he maintained a growing friendship with the drug dealer's girlfriend which noticeably irritated the drug dealing boyfriend; who was by that time being told things by his girlfriend that would eventually place our client in imminent danger.

The client remonstrated that on a bright sunny Saturday morning during a peaceful time when he was sitting behind his trailer enjoying the day, the neighbour and his girlfriend exited their trailer during a heated argument. Coming to the rear of their unit and directly beside where our client was sitting, the boyfriend began berating his girlfriend and accusing her of having an affair with the neighbour. It was evident to my client that the drug dealer was building up to a raging conflict, which generally happened three or four times a week; a rage indicative of drug abuse and addiction. The increasingly enraged boyfriend grabbed a large ball peen hammer and started threating to bash in the head of our client who was attempting to avoid eye contact. The boyfriend dropped the hammer, went back into his trailer and the girlfriend raced off in the white van. Thinking the situation was over; our client moved his chair closer to the creek and tried to put the incident out of his mind.

Within minutes, the raging boyfriend stormed outside with a 38 revolver pistol, rushed up to our client, waved the gun around in the air and pushed him over in his chair, threatening that he was going to blow his head off because he was sleeping with his girlfriend. At this point, my client says that he got up from the ground and, while trying to placate the out of control neighbour, started walking north past the rear of the drug dealers' trailer.

Before he could clear the area and, still within about ten feet of where the initial argument had taken place earlier, the enraged male ran after our client and shoved the gun into his face.

The next few minutes as relayed by the client changed the rest of his life as he explained that in an absolute state of fear, precipitated by the out of control lunatic waving a gun in his face, he grappled with the assailant and, in total fear for his life, struck the assailant's hand and knocked the gun to the ground. As the assailant was struggling to retrieve the fire arm, the client says that he scrambled around on the ground and saw the large hammer lying in the dirt.

Fearing for his life he grabbed the hammer, stood up and swung the metal head at the shoulders of the aggressor. Unfortunately, the hammer glanced of the man's head and he dropped suddenly to the ground. Not moving and with blood seeping from his skull, my client thought that he was dead and, in fear and confusion knelt down beside the wounded man. Just as he was checking the male for injuries, the assailant woke up, grabbed the handgun and started to aim the gun at our client. Wrestling the gun again from his hand, the client managed to twist the gun sideways, rip the gun out of his hands and in total fear for his life; shot him in the head.

Panicking, the client grabbed the gun, ran up the creek bed a considerable distance and, on the other side of the roadway, recalled throwing the gun into the deepest part of the creek where the reeds and bulrushes covered the bank.

In total confusion and shock, the client said that he ran back around to the front of his trailer, jumped in his vehicle and tore out of the trailer parking lot and drove north on the Island Highway. After a few minutes of driving, the client says that he earlier recalled meeting the owner of the local auto wrecking yard the year before and that he had become acquainted with the owner and, thinking that he could tell his side of the story, drove into the business, met with the owner and blurted out what had just happened at the campground.

In shock and dazed, my client said that he left the auto wrecking lot and drove back to the trailer park whereas the police arrested him coming into the park. He was subsequently charged with second degree murder, convicted and sentenced to 15 years in a federal medium security institution.

Returning to my office and going over all the evidence and exhibits, it was noted that the handgun was never found and that the written statements of the auto wrecker acquaintance, the victim's girlfriend and statements of other tenants in the trailer park were inconsistent.

Compelling was the fact that the handgun was never found, rumours that the decedent's girlfriend had hidden over a hundred thousand dollars of drug money and, the fact that the victim's girlfriend had left before the shooting brought a glimmer hope to the appellant's case. Making a plan of action, it became imperative that verification of the witness statements, finding the handgun and locating the drug money were top priority.

The first positive source of information was that the blonde-haired girlfriend had bragged to our client that she had a storage locker near the campground where she had been hiding drugs and money: in the event that she had to leave the country in a hurry.

The aim was to attend and interview the witnesses. This was not a difficult task, as I knew some of the people involved and felt confident that I would be able to obtain new statements. Not surprisingly, several of the statements indicated different recollections from eight years earlier. In contrast, the statement of the auto wrecker witness was not clear and, it was suggested that maybe that statement may have been subjective in nature and, in the heat of the moment, that the witness had misunderstood our client's confused recollections of the facts. The positive thing was that I personally knew the man who had provided the statement and knew him to be an honest and God-fearing person. However; my advice to that witness was to search his heart and see if maybe he had heard something that was not really intended. In that regards, I am very clear of my understanding of the law and know, without a doubt, that obstruction of justice is a serious offence and made it clear to that particular witness that I was not suggesting my version of the statement but rather advising him to be clear in his communication and "stick to the facts only" when testifying at the appeal trial.

Several years before meeting my client at William Head Institution, our company had opened a small storefront office in the mini mall that housed the storage unit office, several miles north of the campground, across from the auto wrecking yard and north of the appellant's previous campground.

Knowing the storage unit management from being a former tenant, I attended at the facility and learned that the former owners had sold the business several years earlier and had left the country. After learning this fact, I enquired with the new managers and asked if they were aware of any storage units that had been abandoned about nine years earlier.

The new manager of the storage unit immediately recognized my name and said that she had met one of my relatives recently and knew that I was an investigator. It was a good lead, and I was praying that they would cooperate and search through their old and delinquent records. Staying for a cup of coffee, the manager's wife, who had made the connection to my daughter, brought a dusty old countertop box into the room and began searching through the outdated records.

Voila! The contact found an 8 x 10 storage unit that had been abandoned years earlier and, according to the file card, the lock was still on the unit - as the new managers were still in the process of trying to organize and sort out the client roster which they had inherited from the previous owners.

My excitement was absolutely uncontrollable as I asked for the name of the client who had originally rented the storage unit. No surprise, the name and address was that of the deceased man's girlfriend. My next question was if the new managers would be willing to cut the lock off the storage unit so that I could take a look inside. With bated breath, I waited for the coveted answer.

"Well, I guess" was the hesitant response.

My response was: "I'll go and get my camera."

Walking with the manager to the abandoned unit; which happened to be at the far end of a middle row of storage units, the manager cut off the old and rusty lock. When I pulled up the sliding door of the storage unit, there, in the far corner, was a six-foot wooden table filled with stacks of 50 and 100 dollar bills. In addition, we observed numerous packets of a white powered substance, which I believed to be cocaine.

Turning to the storage unit manager, I asked her to phone the police while I took photographs of the money and drugs. Having not set foot in the storage unit, we closed the door and waited for the RCMP to arrive.

Approximately fifteen minutes later a male police officer who I casually knew, arrived at the storage locker, looked inside, closed the door and took our written statements. While providing my statement, I advised the police officer that I had taken several photographs of the table and contents and, provided him the name of the lawyer who had hired my services. Obtaining a file number from the officer, I gave him my business card.

Renewed with the exhilaration of finding the money and the drugs, I set out to find the handgun that had not been located. Unfortunately, my search did not locate the handgun in the creek; however, I understand years later the gun was in fact found.

Finishing the investigation and sensing

that the defence lawyer had a solid case for trial, we headed to court. Although not privy to all the evidence provided at trial, I was called in as an expert witness and testified to the court about re-interviewing the witnesses and finding the cash and drugs in the abandoned storage locker. It was sufficient evidence to create reasonable doubt and establish to the jury that our client had acted in self defense when the drug dealer attacked him with the hammer and handgun.

Several weeks later the trial was over and the jury retired to deliberate and, wanting to be in the courtroom when the jury returned, I requested a telephone call when court was reconvened. Not surprisingly, the jury rendered a decision of not guilty that afternoon. It was a rewarding moment to hear the trial judge say to our client:

"Sir, you have been found innocent of the charges against you and are free to leave this courtroom. Is there anything you wish to say to the court?"

Surprisingly, our client responded:

"Your honour, can I be escorted back to the prison to collect my personal items?"

Whereas the honourable trial judge said with a bemused look on his face:

"Sir, after spending eight years in a federal prison do you honestly feel that you need to return to the institution and retrieve a few personal items?"

Whereas our elated client replied: "No, not really your honour."

And the anticipated response from the Judge: "Good decision, sir! You are free to leave."

CHAPTER 19

Surveillance Case #3

In the summer of 1999, when we were clearing three acres of land beside a large provincial campground on Lake Cowichan, we were both retained by a stock broker to conduct surveillance on a client of his who had hired our client to assist a young man with obtaining a significantly large inheritance. The details of the case were that the acquaintance, a 24-year-old self-professed entrepreneur and an only child, had been born in Europe and was described as a wild spending, globetrotting heir who had lived all over the world and whose mother had recently died and bequeathed him 25 million dollars on his 25th birthday.

The saga went on to say that before the heir could receive the inheritance, which was being managed in trust by his Aunt Tia from New Mexico, the heir nephew had to liquidate five million dollars in personal debts that were outstanding in England, Canada and the United States. Furthermore, the names of the creditors were somewhat obscure and referred to things like *Sea Side Pharmaceuticals*, and a host of other nonsensical names.

Our client appeared to be a wealthy 30 something male that was assisting his client in securing quick money to pay off the debts so that he could prove to his aunt that he was being responsible and capable of managing his deceased mother's vast estate. The plan that the nephew had brought to our client, was that he was willing to write a promissory note for borrowing, as an investment, large amounts of cash to pay out the debts he owed; with the promise to promptly pay back the investors' amounts with a return yield of up to 300 percent interest on their investment. The average amount was $15,000 to $20,000 but went as high a $150,000. Believing that their investment was easy money, the list of investors came from every walk of life. The list documented the names of lawyers, doctors, homeowners, school teachers, police officers, a judge and various other working class people who invested in *The Draw* as it was named: for a quick profit with absolutely no income tax encumbrances. The thought of the concept was pure genius, and no one was the wiser. There was also a suggestion that our client had invested his 85 year old mother's money to the tune of $90,000.

It was also evident that our client, who did not want to sign a formal contract with us, paid all his bills and our retainer in cash. On our first meeting, the client handed me a bag full of cash to the sum of $10,000 for approximately two weeks of surveillance to be conducted by my wife and myself.

Being held to a higher standard and in compliance with the *Code of Ethics* required by Private Investigators licenced under the *Security Agencies Act*, I provide the client a receipt for the cash - written on the back of one of my business cards; which was something that I did on occasion if my receipt book was not available.

The client took the card, stuck it in his pocket and commenced to give us a description of the surveillance subject as being: 24-years-old, dark skinned, five foot nine inches tall, with shoulder length dark curly hair and brown eyes. He also described his client as slim in build, dignified looking and well dressed.

We were also told that the subject and his aunt were predisposed to fine dining and travelling around the world; which consequentially made them unavailable on short notice. In addition, our client told us that he had been hired by the young man and that his client's aunt managed the liquidation of his bills so that the beneficiary could inherit millions of dollars on his next birthday. A birth date that was never provided but adroitly side stepped when the question came up in conversation.

Exercising due diligence, I asked our client for a photograph of the subject and a copy of the promissory notes that had been provided to the investors. Not surprisingly, it was difficult obtaining a copy of the contracts and a photograph of the subject was never provided, despite numerous requests.

Over the next six months, my partner and I conducted hundreds of hours of surveillance, travel time and incidental expenses in an attempt to obtain a still photograph of the subject and, an attempt to videotape his activities; having not seen the subject on any surveillance occasions. The *modus operandi* of our client was to phone our office at the oddest times throughout the day and blurt out in a rushed and anxious manner: "The heir and his aunt are meeting some new investors at 6:00 p.m. tonight in the restaurant" or wherever the subject was supposed to be at that given time and "we need you to conduct surveillance".

Racing off from either our office or personal residence, with little or no notice, was stressful in the least. However, every two weeks our wealthy client, who always seemed to have a brown bag full of cash in his sports jacket pocket, kept paying our services in $100 bills.

Within the first month my partner and I had each conducted over one hundred hours of surveillance and travel, which came to over ten thousand dollars in billed fees. Again, for each cash payment I continued to provide the client a signed receipt on the back of my business card.

Our client was not aware that we had been depositing the cash into our corporate bank account and recording the cash income in the monthly income and expense register. As the months went on and the surveillance intensified, our client began grumbling that his acquaintance was inconsistent, obscure in nature and very seldom stayed in one place for very long.

On one particular evening in the early fall, our client phoned me at the very last minute of the working day and advised that the heir was meeting him for dinner at an out of town restaurant and, could both Gloria and I, rush to the restaurant, hide in the bushes by the front door and get a few photographs of his client when he left the restaurant and also follow him after the meeting.

Once again, we dashed out, set up for surveillance near the designated restaurant and watched the area for over four hours; without seeing any sign of the male or his Aunt Tia, who was described as middle-aged, dark complexioned, dark haired and exquisitely dressed with an aura of wealth and breeding.

Becoming annoyed with our client's

constant demands to "jump through" all the hoops of watching for hours without any results, I called the client on my cell phone and asked where he was. His response was that he had only stayed at the restaurant for a few minutes as his client *sensed* that he was being watched and that they left together. When I questioned the sense of that particular statement, he replied that he thought we had seen him leaving, had taken some pictures and followed him to where he was staying. I knew at that time that our client was not being truthful as we had been in our surveillance position long before he was supposed to arrive. Being frustrated by the conflicting information, we departed the area.

Confronting the client and telling him that we were finished with our surveillance and closing the file, the client lamented that it was really important that we continue our surveillance, as the beneficiary had nearly paid off all his debts and that the investors were close to getting their money.

At my protestations, the client became visibly agitated, begged us to stay on the job so that he would not lose his investment, reached into his sports coat pocket and handed me another ten thousand dollars in cash and asked if I would stay on the case for another month. I took the money, gave him a business card receipt and left for the night.

Over the next ten days we heard nothing from our client; however, on the 11th day, at around four twenty p.m., I received a phone call from a pay phone somewhere on Vancouver Island. In a loud and contrived voice, which I believed to be the voice of our client, he repeatedly referred to me by my full name asking when I intended on paying him back the $10,000 that I had borrowed from him 11 days ago. It was obvious that the conversation was being recorded and responded that I had not borrowed any money from him and that I would be providing him a full accounting of our services to date, in writing, over the next 24 hours.

After hanging up the phone and mulling over the odd conversation for several hours that evening, I called a retired judge friend of mine and shared with him the details of the phone call earlier that day. He advised me to prepare a full reconciliation in writing of all our expenses and, if there was any money owing from the cash deposits, then I should mail the client a cheque in that amount. Before ending the conversation, I advised my friend that we had deposited all the cash received from the client into our corporate bank account.

The next morning, I prepared a four page invoice and a full reconciliation of the past six months of services, expenses, fees and sundry disbursements and wrote a cheque in the amount of the credit owed to the client from the entire amount of money that he had given us from the onset of being hired.

Making a copy of the invoice, I mailed the document and cheque to the client's last known address. To my utter joy, the cheque was cashed within six days and I never spoke with him again. When the cheque cleared our bank account we knew that we had been played and suspected that the beneficiary and his wealthy aunt did not exist, although we had been operating in good faith.

Several years later we read in the newspaper that our former client had been charged under the *British Columbia Securities Commissions Act* with fraud and sentenced to a federal institution.

CHAPTER 20

Criminal Case #6
The "Wonky Eye"

Around the same time that I was investigating a religious cult in the interior of British Columbia, near the United States border, I received a telephone call from a lawyer client who asked me to meet with his client regarding a domestic situation. The case involved accusations against his client whereby her estranged husband accused his wife of taking drugs and being an unfit mother.

Meeting with the young mother in a restaurant, I was shocked at how thin and emaciated the woman looked, and my heart went out to her as she related how her eldest daughter had told her that she had seen her father crushing pills into her mother's speciality drink, early one evening. Simultaneously, the young mother was experiencing swelling in both eyes, inability to focus for extended periods of time, hand tremors, and thought that she was suffering from thyroid problems. She explained to me, that for the entire week before her daughter had told her what she'd seen, that her husband of eighteen years, completely out of character, had been bringing coffee to her desk while she worked, each morning. It was not until her daughter told her what she'd seen, that she put two and two together, and realized that she was being drugged. She continued that her husband had been prescribed Citalopram due to a chemical imbalance diagnosis – the prescription was meant for him, a 250 pound man – not for her, a 150 pound woman with no history of chemical imbalance. The young mother fretted that it was this drug she had been ingesting. She related that, out of fear for her life, she grabbed the children and fled to her hometown.

Unfortunately, before she could gather herself together, the estranged husband cancelled credit cards held in their joint names, began hiding their considerable assets and had their joint bank accounts frozen.

The next day, the young mother attended a local medical clinic, explained the situation, and provided a urine sample. On the following Tuesday, the family doctor advised her that she had tested positive for GHB (commonly known as a date rape drug) and Citalopram. Her estranged husband used the positive drug test to his advantage, and was now seeking full custody of their children. The young mother was devastated and wanted to know if I would take her case and prove her innocent. I willingly obliged and obtained a release of information from the client.

Attending at the downtown laboratory, I presented my credentials and told the manager of the clinic that I needed to know the chain of custody for a particular sample that had been provided by my client on Friday afternoon. After an hour of waiting, I was informed that only the administrator in the Vancouver head office could release that information and that my name and phone number had been provided to the head office.

Providing my business card, I departed the clinic not expecting to hear from the organization again. However, the following day I received a phone call from the Vancouver lab whereas a manager wanted to confirm the details of my request. She was told that it was imperative that my client acquire proof of the *Chain of Custody* of the specimen collected, and that the information was to be provided in writing.

The laboratory contact told me that she had investigated the specimen handling and that there had been a problem with the *Chain of Custody* and that the specimen had been left out on the counter late Friday afternoon and not placed in the fridge before the staff left that evening. In addition, she lamented that the specimen had been left on the counter all weekend and not discovered until Monday morning, sent to the lab in Vancouver and tested positive for GHB.

Requesting confirmation of the break in the *Chain of Custody* and the mishandling of the specimen, I thanked the manager for being candid and, not surprisingly, she retorted that the patient had been responsible for placing the specimen in the fridge available to the public, and that the lab would not take responsibility for the oversight.

Not accepting that explanation resultant of the duress, stress and concerns of my client at that time, I required confirmation that the specimen had in fact tested positive for GHB. Again, I was advised that the specimen had tested positive for GHB. In response, I told the manager that GHB is an airborne drug and that a specimen left on a counter, uncovered over the weekend, could invariably test positive.

The manager reluctantly agreed with that assertion and I again demanded that a copy of the results; indicating conclusively that there had been no *Chain of Custody* of the specimen and, the fact that GHB would show positive if the specimen were left out on a counter in the open air. She reluctantly agreed to write those facts in a legal letter, document the manner in which the testing had been mishandled and email those facts to my office the following day.

Receiving the information from the laboratory the following day, I emailed the results to our client's lawyer and recommended that a petition be made to the court to have the test results overturned and expunged from the client's medical file.

On a sunny May 3rd, two days before our wedding anniversary, I set off for the interior of B.C. seeking answers as to why the well-established and senior manager of the local public works department had drugged his young and beautiful wife. His sworn affidavits filed with the court system portrayed him as nothing less than an entirely sober, devoted, loving husband and father, and my course was set on proving otherwise.

Upon arriving in the interior, locating a motel room and going over my file notes, I commenced inquiries. From years of experience as a gumshoe, I knew that the local pub was the best place to start. Parking my vehicle in an obscure place, in case surveillance became necessary at a later time, I walked the quaint and historic main street of the small town.

Standing on a sunny street corner and, turning my head in a 360-degree cursory scan, I located three hotels that boasted beer parlours and lounges on the main street.

Choosing what appeared to be the most popular bar in town, I strolled into the cocktail lounge and ordered a coffee from the attractive female engaging and flirting with the bar flies who as regulars, knew everyone and everything.

There were times when I struggled to look like a local yokel; however; my trade mark attire was generally brown leather shoes, beige slacks, cream coloured open necked shirt and a matching sports jacket; the antithesis of innocuous surveillance clothes. To say the least, I looked like a dude or a retired cop. To add another aura of mystique; I wore a military belt buckle that was obvious with the open sports coat. On my lapel were generally two regimental pins further heralding that I was a veteran of some foreign wars. Casually standing at the bar between two raucous men of the world, I caught the eye of the smiling bartender valiantly working the bar patrons for tips.

When I asked for the coffee, the bartender established in seconds that I was not one of the regulars in the small wilderness community. Taking the coffee, I hitched myself onto the bar stool and scanned the place to ensure that the subject of my investigation was not in the bar for lunch hour. Within minutes of taking the first sip of java, the pretty and obviously astute bartender loaded up her tray and sauntered out onto the floor of the lounge.

Being that is was lunch time and Friday afternoon, it was apparent that within fifteen minutes the working class would head back to their offices, as they had come in for the noon hour pub fare meal and would be gone shortly. Having occasionally spent time in pubs around the world during my 12 years of sea time, reading the bar crowd was second nature.

After of a few more minutes between the two unemployed males and, being caught in a crossfire conversation, I left the bar and moved over to a small table in the far corner with my back to the wall: a comfortable place that law enforcement, private investigators and pugilists find secure. My father had trained me in the art of boxing since the age of seven as he had been an Olympic boxer prior to the war.

As the pub started to clear out from the lunch crowd, I noticed the ever-circulating female bartender surreptitiously glancing toward my table; in an attempt to be oblivious to my presence. As I drained the last of the coffee from the mug, the female bartender, who seemed to know everyone and everything about the small town, strolled over to my table and offered a refill, whereby I nodded assent. Not more than 15 minutes later the bartender finished her shift, walked over to my table and, standing to the left side of me asked: "So, what brings you to our small town?"

"Passing through." was my succinct response.

After several more minutes of small talk, she asked what I was really doing in town and was there anything else that I needed at my table. Smiling, I asked how long she had been working in the hotel bar and would she be willing to answer some questions about the real purpose of my being in the establishment.

It was obvious that I was taking a risk in asking questions; however, if I had read her correctly, she was the person in the know. In a soft voice I told her that I was an investigator working on a file in the community.

She immediately responded that she had initially thought that I was either an undercover police officer or some type of investigator. Taking an even bigger risk, I showed her my Private Investigator Licence and asked for her assistance. She agreed and I ventured with the name of the estranged husband that I was presently investigating.

Not surprisingly, she told me that the subject of my inquiries was well known in the pub, not very well liked, and was always hitting on the females in the lounge. I asked her to join me when she got off work. She turned around, walked back to the bar, poured herself a coffee and came back and sat down at my table.

Picking up where we had left off, the contact remonstrated that the subject of my inquiries was not a very nice man and that he recently bragged to some of the female bartenders that he regularly took trips to Bountiful, a small place just this side of the American border, as he was being paid to inseminate young teenage girls, recently married to older men in the colony. She described how the colony was exhibiting birth defects in the offspring from incest breeding: which was manifested as a "lazy eye" in the children, which was being mitigated by the addition of outside genetics.

Instinctively knowing that she was telling the truth, I asked questions about any other local males that she knew who might be part of the breeding scheme. The new contact named several other local males and described how the scheme worked. Apparently, the males would present themselves at the colony and make arrangements with several male leaders of the religious sect; to engage in sexual relations with the young girls in an attempt to breed out the birth defects, locally referred to as "*The wonky eye*".

The verbal contract that was agreed upon was a cash payment, and that the outside males would be supervised by the sect females in a closed off room whereby the male providers would sit on a chair behind a curtain (from the ceiling to their waists) and that the young girls would be escorted into the room and positioned on the lap of the contracted male. The supervised act of insemination was that no touching or talking would be allowed, which was strictly supervised by the female overseers. When the act was completed, the males were paid and escorted off the property.

Having learned what I came to find out, I decided to take a road trip to the colony and thereby personally confirm that child sexual abuse was actually being perpetrated. Thanking the informant, she gave me her word that she would not disclose my investigation and, that if I required anything more she always worked the same shift from opening to late afternoon and took a short break after lunchtime.

Later that afternoon, after the off-duty bartender had left the pub, I checked into a local motel, changed clothes to running shoes, blue jeans, t-shirt, pullover and a ball cap and proceed to the colony, arriving shortly thereafter.

Wanting to give the impression that I was a new source of DNA, I met with one of the male leaders of the colony on the pretext of offering my services and learned that the recently married young girls were only available on certain days, and that I could leave a phone number whereby I would be called at the appropriate time. Thanking them for the information, I left without providing a contact number, explaining that I was travelling through the province.

Returning to the motel, I thought it best to open a police file at the local detachment and, upon arriving at the station met an incredibly professional corporal who opened *An Information* on the subject of my investigation and promised to investigate the allegations about the drugging of his estranged wife. The officer further acknowledged that once his investigation was finished, including the child abuse going on at the colony; he would get back to me about the investigation.

After leaving the police station, I attended at a second bar in the downtown core and learned from that bar staff that the subject of my investigation was not liked, was an alcoholic and currently barred from their drinking establishment.

The following morning, the second day in the small rural town, I conducted a drive past of the subject's property, as detailed by my client and, upon arrival at the residence, noticed a male bearing the description of the subject, standing on the porch of the house talking to a female. They were laughing and drinking beer. As it was Saturday, and the subject was not working, I decided to set up surveillance and see what he was up to over the next ten or twelve hours. He continued to party and spent the next several hours in and around the house in the company of the young female. It was interesting to note the age of the young lady.

Leaving for home the third day, I prepared a report and made an appointment to meet with the client's lawyer. Several days later we met and after presenting the investigative report, the lawyer submitted an Exparte' Order to the court petitioning for sole custody, guardianship and child support. The application was successful and divorce proceedings commenced.

Unfortunately, the charges against the husband were dropped for administering a toxic drug, which was proven to be the prescribed drug Citalopram. This had been an attempt to discredit his wife for the purpose of gaining custody of their children and, ridding himself of his wife so that he could carry on with his perverted activities. As to the deposition of the sexual abuse allegations at the colony, that case went before the Supreme Court of Canada many years later which ultimately contributed to the conviction of several male leaders of the cult.

As a postlude to that heartfelt investigation, I am very pleased to write that the aggrieved young mother and her three children have become the best of friends with my wife and I since first meeting her in 2005, and that this remarkable and talented survivor of domestic abuse recovered from that debilitating trauma, self-actualized, became a well-respected business woman and literary author who I am very proud to know.

CHAPTER 21

Surveillance Case #4

This case was assigned by an adjustor employed by an insurance company client who regularly used our services for surveillance. The claimant was a female who resided on one of the Gulf Islands situated in the inside straights off Vancouver Island. The injuries on file reported by the subject were due to a third party motor vehicle accident resulting in the claimant initiating a Notice of Civil Claim for bodily injury, pain and suffering, loss of income, special damages and loss of enjoyment of life. In addition, the claimant reported that she was unable to work in her profession as a nurse and was claiming considerable wage loss over an extended period of time.

Obtaining all the pertinent details of the injury, litigation claim, limitations of movement resultant of the soft tissue injuries and address and description of the claimant, our female investigator proceeded with the file. Travelling to the claimant's residence, our investigator obtained numerous photographs of the property, house, motor vehicles and other information relevant to the assignment. Setting up in an obscure position to obtain videotape and still photographs, our investigator noted the stately, single family dwelling was situated on a large slopping lot, whereas the front quarter of an acre was rough landscaping interspersed with rocks, uneven ground, weeds and grassy sod.

Within several hours of commencing surveillance, an attractive female, bearing a resemblance to the claimant, exited the home in a bright pink sweat suit and was observed pushing a wheelbarrow and gardening tools while working on the front portion of the terraced property. For the next five or six hours, the claimant was observed engaged in heavy landscaping activities on the long sloping terrain. She was observed picking up and relocating large rocks and removing heavy chunks of sod and tossing them into the wheelbarrow. Over a course of several hours the claimant dumped the wheelbarrow full of dirt and sod at various locations throughout the property. In addition, she threw the rocks under a large pine tree at the side of the driveway. Shortly before lunch a male arrived and went into the house.

At lunch time the claimant and her male companion sat on a bench in the front of the house and enjoyed a meal together. This was an important piece of evidence, as the claimant had told the insurance company that she was unable to do any chores around the house because of her injuries, and relied upon her husband to take over household and outdoor responsibilities. The couple interacted in a relaxed, cheerful and intimate manner and we deemed that the male was in fact her spouse. This was also crucial information because the claimant had insinuated a complete breakdown in the marital relationship. After the lunch break, the male went back into the house and the claimant continued her heavy gardening work for several more hours.

On the second day of surveillance, the attractive gardener came outside wearing a bright blue sweat suit and commenced landscaping where she had left off the day before. With the wheelbarrow tilted length ways on the uneven front terraced hillside, the claimant bent over and, on her hands and knees, commenced cutting sod out of the ground which she then tossed into the wheelbarrow.

On videotape and still photographs, the claimant was observed bending over, cutting out sod, lifting the heavy chunks and throwing them through the air into the wheelbarrow. After another long afternoon of cutting sod, removing rocks and leveling the uneven ground while using a shovel and rake, the claimant returned into the house.

On day three, the claimant came outside mid-morning dressed in a bright yellow sweat suit and recommenced landscaping where she had left off the afternoon before. The claimant continued the heavy landscaping activities throughout the day and departed in a van at dinnertime with a friend. A decision was made not to pursue the claimant at that time and our investigator ceased surveillance activities.

Over the three days of observation, our investigator obtained more than 18 hours of videotape of the claimant involved in heavy landscaping activities and, obtained more than 20 four by six supplementary coloured photographs showing the claimant digging sod, throwing the sod through the air into a wheelbarrow and hurling rocks to the side of the terraced front yard.

When presenting the evidence, it was well-established what day the claimant was working by the colour of the sweat suits. In fact, our report referred to the pink day, the blue day and the yellow day. The courts require three consecutive days of activity in a bodily injury file so that the claimant is not able to say that they worked on day one, felt sore and tired on day two and attempted again to work on day three. This was crucial evidence as the claimant physically toiled for three consecutive days; wearing different coloured sweat suits each day, conclusively establishing her physical strength and level of fitness.

It was an amazing collection of evidence and the videotape and complimentary photographs became an insurance standard which was indicative of the superior calibre of professionalism on the part of our investigator.

CHAPTER 22

Surveillance Case #5

Having successfully completed our first child protection case the year prior in the Fraser Valley of British Columbia, a law firm contacted our office and expressed concern regarding a court order allowing a seven-year-old boy, who was in the care of his maternal grandmother, to be permitted a 21 day visit at his mother's home in the interior; however, there were strict conditions imposed on the monitored visit regarding the mother's aberrant sexual behavioural patterns with regards to pornographic websites. The court ordered conditions were that the child was not to be in the same room as his mother if the mother was on a computer or laptop. In fact, the mother was directed by the court order to cease all computer activity while the child was awake and, particularly in the evening before bed. In addition, the child was to be monitored for aggressive behaviour patterns. A breach of the court order could result in the apprehension of the child by Social Services.

The challenge of having eyes on the

mother during the day and until the child went to bed posed considerable logistical maneuvering and in that regard, our female investigator was required to follow the mother and the child from the time of handover and pursue them to the mother's apartment and conduct surveillance while the child was awake. In addition, the mother and child were to be followed whenever they left the apartment.

Upon arriving in the vicinity of the mother's second story apartment, and after locating an ideal surveillance point from which the living room, kitchen and dining room were visible, surveillance commenced. An interesting point about conducting surveillance is that *Privacy Act Legislation* in the Province of British Columbia differs from the *Federal Privacy Act,* and each province maintains different legislation regarding expectation to privacy, trespassing and retrieving discarded refuse.

In British Columbia it is a breach of the *Provincial Privacy Act* to trespass on a subject's property, obtain videotape through a covered window, and climb a tree or building on the subject's property and through any means not legal within the *Federal Privacy Act*. For example, the most opportune time to obtain videotape is in the dark and through a back lit window or patio door. If the curtains are not closed there is no expectation to privacy.

Again, the act of obtaining evidence is mandated by a reasonable expectation to privacy. With regards to *dumpster diving*, an expression used by investigators, it is known that anything discarded from the property such as a garbage bag or can placed on public property can be retrieved by the investigator; as the refuse is deemed to have been abandoned. It is amazing what reasonable people throw in garbage bags: envelopes, bank statements, shopping lists, medical appointments and other information that would assist an investigator to precede a subject to their destination, which decreases and limits detection. Many a criminal and civil case has been solved as a result of "*dumpster dives*." Latex gloves are a handy tool in this endeavour.

Regarding the mother and her seven-year-old child, everything seemed to be normal the first two or three days; however, after a quiet day with her son, the subject suffered a relapse one evening and failed to adhere to the court order after dark. Fortunately for our investigator, all the lights were on inside the apartment and the windows were not covered, which greatly enhanced surveillance opportunities. Furthermore, the subject had set her computer station up on the dining room table which afforded our investigator the opportunity to videotape, observing the activity over the mother's shoulder and capture, on video tape, what was being displayed on the monitor. The breach of the court order established that the seven-year-old child was standing by his mother and looking at the computer monitor. Another major breach of the court order was that the child was not supposed to be in the same room during that viewing, which was sufficient evidence to report the activity and apprehend the child.

The mother of this child was addicted to chat rooms and pornography sites where perverse sexual activity was being displayed through a skype monitor. The site was also a *sadism and masochism* site whereby the subject (mother of the child) used a pseudonym name which referred to being whipped and beaten during sexual activity. This information came from the fact that we needed to advise the client's lawyer of the website domain for evidentiary purposes, or the mother's behaviour would continue and the child would be exposed to the aberrant behaviour.

In that regard, I was required to log into the domain chat room, which information was relayed to me by our female investigator during surveillance activities, so that I could engage with the subject in a sting operation. This was successful and on completion of several such documented "stings", I reported my findings to the client's lawyer and swore an affidavit as to what was going on with the child's mother. I found this very distasteful; however, the child's wellbeing was of paramount concern.

The court was very aware of the necessity of surveillance and monitoring of the child's behaviour, as whenever the child was in his mother's care and custody, the child exhibited a complete change of personality at which times he displayed unpredictable behaviour, flashes of rage and inappropriate sexual acting out.

Our investigator observed that when the child was playing alone in the street, or walking alone to school, he would suddenly spin around, leap in the air and make karate like gestures while grimacing like a maniac. After his arrival at school the child was observed and documented (by note taking, as cameras are not permitted near school grounds) during recess and lunch activities. The child displayed aggressive humping behaviour while bending over the backs of other children. In addition, he climbed a monkey bar apparatus and commenced foaming at the mouth and spitting on the other children nearby. The other children ran away at the onset of this repulsive behaviour.

After approximately a week of surveillance, our investigator noticed these things happening more often and, through our verbal report to the legal client, the lawyer filed an Exparte' Order to the court for immediate apprehension of the child.

In addition, our investigator was required to cease surveillance, attend in court and give testimony on the witness stand. At a break in the closed hearing, our investigator overheard the child's mother on a pay telephone, telling her mother (the child's grandmother) to get over to her apartment as soon as possible and remove the computer from the premises. Overhearing the conversation, our investigator reported the conspiracy to the court and the court immediately ordered that the local sheriff's department promptly attend and confiscate the computer and monitor. Coincidentally, the sheriff arrived at the apartment at the same time as the grandmother and, the computer and monitor were seized.

Timing was of the essence in that particular situation and, the evidence provided to the family court resulted in the mother losing custody and access to the child and the boy's paternal grandmother being given full guardianship.

CHAPTER 23

Domestic Civil Case #1

During the Christmas break of 2005, the parents of a 38 year old single mother and elementary school teacher, called our offices and shared, in a discrete manner, that they were concerned for their daughter who had told them on Christmas day that she had met this handsome, wealthy and charming man in the United States and, that after a two week whirlwind relationship they had gotten married, and that her new husband had invited their daughter and her 14-year-old son to live in his multi-million dollar beachfront mansion in Washington State. During that conversation the parents told me that their daughter expressed excitement about her new life in the United States and that she had recently resigned her teaching position and would be moving to her new home in early January.

After spending a few weeks with her husband, the new wife began noticing odd things happening in the mansion while the new husband was at work. Not wanting to believe anything would burst this pink bubble, her daughter came to the home of her parents for a few days between Christmas and New Year's and shared concerns about her recent marriage.

Arranging a meeting at the parent's home and speaking with the daughter, who was initially reluctant to open enquires on her new husband, she began disclosing some details of his behaviour.

At that meeting, I offered to open a file and conduct a few background enquiries on the subject. The prospective client was concerned that she might be imagining the strange things that were happening in her life. She shared that after about four days in the 10,000 square foot mansion, while the husband was travelling on business; several young females with new born babies came to the home, introduced themselves to her and told her that they needed to put something in the downstairs deep freezer. Following them down stairs, she observed the young mothers placing numerous bottles of breast milk in the deep freeze. Not wanting to offend the young ladies, our client said that she dismissed the odd activities as maybe friends of her husband who had nowhere to live. However, the young mothers hugged her before leaving and welcomed her into the family. The disconcerting fact that the young ladies were in their early twenties further disturbed the client.

Convinced that something was not right,

the distraught woman made a decision to hire me to conduct a discreet background on her American husband. Before leaving with sufficient information and notes to start a file, my new client stated that she was going back to the mansion the next day and would be back in Canada in about two weeks.

Arriving back at the office, I contacted a former United States naval officer from Dana Point, California who I had met years before when visiting San Diego while serving on the Canadian Navy Destroyer Escort *HMCS Columbia*.

After retiring from the US Navy, my friend started a private investigations business specializing in intelligence gathering. He was an awesome investigator and I subcontracted him to run a complete search on the American subject of my investigation.

Getting involved in something else for about a week, I was surprised to receive a telephone call from my colleague in California who advised that he was in the process of emailing a fourteen-page document about the subject.

He went on to say that the recently acquired husband of my unsuspecting client was currently married to 21 different women and that between the women, there were 36 children sired by her husband and that he owned dozens of expensive mansions throughout the United States, was registered as a real estate broker and had amassed a net worth of 16 million dollars.

My contact further stated that he had run the names and family backgrounds of the 21 young women and found out that they were members of a religious cult and that the full history of all their families, children and relatives was available from the Mormon Church in Salt Lake City, Utah. He suggested that the information was of great concern and required further investigation. I ended the conversation by assigning further background searches on the subject and he agreed to send me the work in progress files.

Reading the fourteen-page document in addition to the notes created by the investigator, it was more than evident that it would take me hours to decipher the family tree of the 21 wives and 36 children. Creating a wall chart, I transposed the family tree of the wives, their children, parents and place of birth. In addition, I separated the professions of the wives and created an additional chart on the real estate holdings of the subject of my investigation.

It was mind boggling to say the least as it unfolded page by page. The subject spent most of his time travelling and buying large mansions throughout the United States, of which the mansion in Washington State was a recent purchase to add to the list of dozens of other such mansions he had purchased over the past few years. Researching the locations where the other mansions were, we located large expensive properties in six mid-western states including Idaho, Utah, Colorado and Washington State. The properties were all listed in corporate names which indicated millions of dollars had been invested. The man we were investigating was obviously a representative of the colony. In addition, it became evident that the subject was buying property closer to the Canadian border and, had recently purchased a mansion in the Creston area of British Columbia, associated with Bountiful: a place where a concerted investigation was being conducted on several child abuse cases involving the Bountiful Polygamist Sect. A file that I had been involved with several years earlier.

My contact in Dana Point California had also done a genealogy report complete with print-out and family trees for all the wives of the subject of my investigation. The mind boggling part was that it appeared that the majority of the children had multiple siblings through their mother who was married to the same male leader in the colony.

It was a genetic web of half-brother and

half-sister relationships living with multiple families that would take days to sort out: if that were even possible without DNA testing.

Conferring with my client during her next visit to Canada and, showing her the results of the investigation, she immediately understood her role in the mansion, which had been prompted by an earlier conversation with her new husband; whereby he recently told her that the role she would assume was that of taking over the education cell of the children who were now showing up at the mansion.

In addition to the new husband advising his most recent wife of her role in the family dynamics, he started becoming more dominant and aggressive with both herself and her teenage son and, when my client resisted, he threatened her with physical harm and punctuated the threat by stating that he had guns in the house and would repel any and all manner of resistance - from within and outside of the organization.

After advising my client to cease all communication with the mansion, her husband and the colony, I recommended that she immediately contact a lawyer and commence proceedings to have the marriage annulled. She agreed and never returned to the mansion although her husband phoned, texted and sent threatening messages to her family in Canada.

Being a certified member of the Council of International Investigators, whose headquarters are in Washington State, I made a call to Homeland Security advising them that there was an arsenal of assault weapons at the address of my client's former husband's mansion. Within sixty days my client was divorced and living quietly in Canada.

As a conclusion to this case, I received a telephone call years later from my former client who shared her gratitude for having literally saved her son and herself. It was a touching moment and even more heartfelt when the former client identified herself and asked: "Do you remember me?"

My choked response was: "Yes of course, I will never forget you or your son."

CHAPTER 24

Civil Investigation Case #4
Project L.U.C.I.D

In the middle of August 1997, I received a phone call from a soft spoken female who refused to identify herself and asked if I would be willing to leave my office, go to a phone booth and call her at a designated phone number in another city on Vancouver Island.

Leaving the office and making the phone call from a pay phone, I asked the speaker the purpose of the clandestine call. In a hesitant and cryptic manner, she told me that she wanted to hire me as an investigator on a personal matter but was afraid to speak on a traceable phone. After hearing the details of the assignment, I agreed to meet her at the public address provided and, before disconnecting the phone, asked the prospective client how I would be able to identify her at the meeting. She responded that she would have a green scarf covering her entire head and would be wearing large square shaped sunglasses.

Two hours later, I parked my vehicle in a parkade several blocks from the pre-arranged spot and, while walking along the sidewalk of a main artery in the downtown core of the city, noticed a short female wearing dark slacks, dark sweater and a green scarf wrapped around her head. She was indeed wearing huge square lens sunglasses and I approached the female. She was sitting at an outside table on the sidewalk in front of a busy restaurant. Sitting down across from the oddly dressed woman, I identified myself and quickly displayed my investigator's licence. I was taken aback by her attire by virtue of the fact that she was totally dressed in winter clothing although it was a hot August afternoon.

The conversation that took place within minutes of sitting down forever changed her life. The prospective client said that she was in serious physical danger and needed to know if she could trust me to be discreet about what she was going to disclose. Without hesitation I assured her that she had an expectation to confidentiality and that I was a member, in good standing, of the Council of International Investigators and that our code of ethics and membership were referred to as being elite in the world of investigators. Whispering in a voice that I could barely hear, she told me that she worked for the Ministry of Mental Health and was being harassed by her former employer who had dismissed her from her previous job in

Eastern Canada for charging him with sexual harassment in the workplace. She further went on to say that her former employer was the CEO of a multi-million dollar defence contracting company that manufactured electronic equipment and a special type of alloy used for military aircraft that was being designed by NASA, in a large military base in Florida.

We agreed to move to a more private place and walked to a local park that was screened by large evergreen trees. Finding a secluded bench behind several huge trees, my new client began telling me the details of the recent threats to her life.

Still wrapped up from head to toe, and unable to see her eyes or face, she told me that she had been sexually harassed in the workplace for several months and, when she confronted her employer, who owned the company she worked for, he threatened to destroy her life if she told anyone about his advances.

She painfully lamented that being unable to continue working for the CEO, she made a complaint with the *Human Rights Commission* and that before the file could be opened; her employer denied the charges and dismissed her for incompetence. Being that the former employer was a wealthy and powerful international businessman, he told her that if she continued with her "false" allegations against him, he was going make her life a living hell.

Fearing for her life and knowing that he was associated with the American Defence Ministry, she left the province and moved to British Columbia, eventually securing a job in the mental health industry. She explained that if she pursued the former employer with legal action, she would most likely be fired from her current position and deemed mentally ill herself.

Gaining her trust, she told me that since moving to Vancouver Island some very strange things had started happening in her apartment and while walking on the street; relating to the hearing of voices, music and people speaking directly into her ears - day and night, while no one was near her. In a tearful voice she claimed that the voices were coming from her microwave oven and light sockets and, while walking alone to work she was hearing voices in her head and a soft male voice was telling her that if she did not stop with the allegations against her former boss, she would be killed.

It was definitely a dangerous position she was in and I promised to represent her to the best of my ability. She was fearful, paranoid and kept looking around and upwards to the sky to see if anyone was spying on her. My client, who I will refer to as Mary, shared with me that she had no idea how the voices were being projected into her head and in the kitchen and, other rooms in her apartment. Walking with her to her home six blocks west of where we had met, we went upstairs and checked out the apartment.

For the record, I have experience in sweeping rooms and checking electrical receptacles, cables, and phone boxes where electronic bugs and other devices can be hidden. In that regard, I know that microwave ovens emit electronic emanations at around 30 megahertz and can interfere with electronic devices and create odd noises. Mary was not convinced that there were no electronic or mind control devices in her home and asked that I conduct a thorough examination of her entire apartment.

As Mary's anxiety grew in intensity, I shared with her that I personally knew a retired United States Airforce Captain by the name of Texe Marrs who had specialized in electronic warfare, and had formerly worked as an intelligence analysist for the United States Ministry of Defence under the administration of former President George Herbert Walker Bush.

In addition, I advised her that my former military friend was also a professor at the University of Austin, Texas and a renowned author who had written over thirty books, of which his most recent book titled L.U.C.I.D, referred to the ominous Lucifer Trust in New York City.

During our conversation, I told Mary that I personally knew about the book L.U.C.I.D. which details universal human mind control and a covert government operation destined to devour the whole world.

According to Texe, every person on Earth – even newborn babies – will be issued the universal biometric I.D. Card and eventually a microchip containing a UPC (Universal Product Code) identifying that specific individual. Texe had been able to decipher the bar code based on information given to him by an individual who claimed to have received the code sequencing in a dream. It is a fascinating study in universal human intelligence gathering (HUMINT). People who resist the biometric I.D. Card and chip implant will have a mind control biochip surgically implanted into their brains, and the ISO 9000 programs will require that all manufactured goods be controlled with a UPC number. The first three digits of the individual UPC will be six hundred and sixty-six (666). This is the International Number and is referred to, in Biblical Scriptures, as the number of the Beast. The next three digits will be a National Number followed by a Regional three digit Number and then, finally the individual's nine digit Social

Security Number. To this end even infants are being issued SIN Numbers.

The eighteen digit Number will clearly identify each person on earth and track all of their transactions. Project L.U.C.I.D. will empower a One World Order to control all individuals who take the Mark of the Beast contained in the injected microchip.

According to Texe, America's hidden SS establishment will use its massively powerful computer databases to control bank accounts, purchases, and to monitor our every move (extracts from the book L.U.C.I.D., first published on September 1st, 1996).

After securing a retainer from Mary, I agreed to do more research on the matter and get back to her in a few days. In the interim, I told her not to speak out loud in her apartment and refrain from using the microwave oven until we could converse again.

Back at the office, I phoned my friend Texe Marrs in Austin, Texas and shared with him what my client Mary had told me about the voice projections in her ears on the street and in her apartment. Texe was delighted that I had called him and invited me to visit his home in Texas.

Calling the client, I informed her that I had a credit with American Airlines from a cancelled trip to the last Council of International Investigators Conference in Los Angeles, and that I would be going to Texas for a few days to meet with Texe Marrs.

Booking a flight out of Seattle, Washington and a ferry vehicle space on the Seattle Clipper out of Victoria, British Columbia, I boarded the ferry at 10:00 a.m. on a sunny August day arriving at the Seattle Ferry Terminal at approximately 12:45 p.m. Driving to SeaTac International Airport, I checked my vehicle into long term parking and boarded an American Airlines flight destined for Austin, Texas via Denver, Colorado; arriving in Austin at 7:10 p.m.

Checking into a hotel within the hour of arriving in Austin and, after getting settled in for the evening, I called Texe at his home and made arrangements to meet him at his office later the next morning. Renting a car the following day, I drove south to the famous Bee Caves area of Austin, Texas close to where Texe operated his business *Living Truth Ministries.* The weather was beautiful and I made good time driving to the appointment.

Arriving at his office, I spent the next hour being introduced to Texe's staff and going over his extensive operation. We were both retired military officers and it was wonderful to share personal experiences from the past. Later in the afternoon, Texe presented me a signed copy of his newest book *L.U.C.I.D.* and shared with me his in-depth knowledge of the recent defence contract out of NASA, whereby my client Mary's former employer, who owned an aluminum company, was involved in the testing and experimenting of metals and fuselage coatings that would virtually make American Airforce jets invisible to the human eye and undetectable by radar while soaring around the globe.

Texe also told me that the very same company was doing major research in a mind control method and had recently perfected a system of bouncing air waves and human voices from satellites in space and projecting those voices into human ears: on the street, in buildings and through microwave ovens. Texe further told me that his book *L.U.C.I.D* referred to a Supreme Court case in New York City, where a citizen, a victim of the same mind control activities, had recently won a major lawsuit against the Department of National Defence for invasion of privacy and mind control experimentation. I was excited about the news and made notes in my file.

Spending the night with Texe and his family, I departed their home the following morning and headed south to Corpus Christi; as I wanted to take a trip over to Padre Island in the

Gulf of Mexico and see a former Navy friend. The day was beautiful and as I drove south on US Route 77, fond memories of military days of yore brought back waves of nostalgia.

However, shortly before noon on August 31st while travelling south in blissful contentment at having obtained empowering evidence for my client in Canada, the barometer dropped significantly and the sky turned ominously black.

Sensing the rain about to fall, and hearing a roar of wind, the sky opened in a torrent of blowing rain. Within minutes, the highway was awash and I saw a tractor trailer several hundred feet behind my vehicle sliding sideways down the freeway in the outside lane. Concerned about the compact rental car withstanding the roaring wind, I drove under an overpass and pulled over to the west side of the highway.

For approximately 15 minutes the rain slashed at the vehicles struggling to stay on the flooding highway. Turning on the vehicle radio, I learned that I was at the edge of Hurricane Dolly which was heading northeast towards Oklahoma. Venturing out of the overpass I shot down the highway toward Corpus Christi and, two hours later, still in the middle of pouring rain, entered Corpus Christi where the famous Gulf Coast Greyhound Race Track sits on the Gulf of Mexico. Driving into the huge parking lot I noticed palm trees blowing back and forth in the wind.

Parking the vehicle, running into the race track lobby and looking up at the noisy large T.V. screen above the main lobby dining room; I read the now famous headlines telling the world that Princess Diana had been killed in an automobile crash in France. The time was approximately 4:31 p.m. and, as a Canadian and son of a British war bride and second generation British subject on my father's side, I was shocked at the news. Within minutes conspiracy theories were flying around the lobby and lounge and everyone was blaming the Queen. It was quite a distraction from the hurricane and, as suddenly as it started, the rain stopped and the sun appeared on the edge of the black clouds.

Thinking that I had outrun Dolly, I decided to try my hand at Greyhound dog racing as my maternal grandfather in England used to race Greyhound dogs; which I remembered as a child in 1954 while visiting my mother's family in Gatwick, England.

After winning four of the first seven races, I decided to leave the sanctuary of the racetrack lounge and take the gulf bridge over to Padre Island. However, half way to the entrance lane for the bridge, I noticed a fleet of shrimp boats coming up under the bridge and executed a hard right turn and drove down under the causeway bridge as the shrimp boats were docking. Fascinated by the unloading of the huge jumbo shrimp, I walked over to the dockside restaurant and got caught up in the excitement of people ordering deep fried jumbo shrimp in a basket. Lining up at the counter and oblivious to the imminent storm, I purchased a huge order of the best shrimp I have ever eaten. Padre Island was forgotten as I wandered around the docks smelling the rich odour of brackish sea water and tidal flats.

As I was getting into the rental car, the wind came up again and the sky turned black. People were racing across the parking lot towards their cars as the rain bounced off the asphalt. Turning on the car radio the news told of another turn in the hurricane which had unwittingly made a twist around from the southwest coast and was racing back up north.

Thinking that it would be wise to leave the area, I headed east out of Corpus Christi on US 1-10 and drove towards New Orleans, Louisiana. Racing along the Gulf Coast with Hurricane Dolly whipping around and behind me, I veered north and started toward the Alabama State Line. Driving for hours in the blowing rain, I reach New Orleans in time to bed down for the night. For nearly three days I outran Hurricane Dolly as I crisscrossed the States of Louisiana, Alabama and Texas. It was four days later that I retrieved my van in Seattle, and catching the ferry returned home to beautiful Vancouver Island.

Meeting the following day with Mary, I shared with her the United States Supreme Court case that Texe Marrs had brought to my attention, and offered to assist her with a civil lawsuit against the Canadian Company operating in the United States. Mary was overwhelmed and I presented her a signed copy of L.U.C.I.D.

A year after filing her petition, Mary successfully negotiated an out of court settlement for wrongful dismissal, invasion of privacy and unlawful use of government technology. It was a huge win and set a precedent in the Supreme Court. Sadly, my friend Texe Marrs passed away on November 23rd, 2019 in Austin, Texas at 75 years of age. Prior to his death, the US Government revoked Texe's non profit designation effectively destroying his Ministry and Outreach; however, the sinister truth had already been published.

CHAPTER 25

Surveillance Case #6

A law firm client that we worked with over the years called our offices late on a Friday afternoon, which was normal in our business, and assigned a surveillance case on young male approximately late 20's or early 30's who had been operating a drug house in a secluded part of the north island. We obtained a full description of the claimant and opened a file. We generally received assignments most weekends and some long weekends as it was an optimal time to conduct surveillance investigations. Over the years my wife and I worked those types of files together so that we could spend time with each other on weekends. In addition, the client got two investigators for the price of one.

This particular case involved a police raid on the drug house in the middle of the night when a thunder flash was thrown through an open window and exploded near the claimant who was sleeping on the floor in the living room. Amid the confusion, yelling of orders to stay down and, by the time the smoke cleared and everyone was rounded up and placed in handcuffs, it was noticed that the young male was missing the lower part of his left arm from the thunder flash that had landed on the floor near his sleeping bag. Screaming in pain, the injured male was transported to hospital and rushed into surgery. Unfortunately, the lower arm from the elbow to the end of his fingers was destroyed in the blast and could not be reattached. As a result of the loss of his arm, a bodily injury claim was filed against the police force by the claimant's lawyer.

Our assignment was to locate the claimant and conduct approximately three days of consecutive surveillance on the subject to establish the effects of the resultant disability. Our client was interested in what the disabled male was capable of doing vis-à-vis his ability to function, quality of life and daily routines. It was a large quantum: meaning the amount of financial exposure to the government; thus, surveillance was necessary to establish the degree of his disability and determine the amount of the settlement.

Locating the claimant in a secluded area of several parcels of small acreages, we proceeded to reconnoitre the area and find a safe viewpoint to observe the house, property and claimant. A long gravel driveway curved in from the main road and traversed approximately three hundred yards toward the house. A large covered porch faced out towards the road and the yard was filled with fruit trees and a few evergreens. The two acre property was wire fenced on three sides with some deciduous and evergreen trees around most of the perimeter. It was ideal for surveillance; however, the most tree coverage was on the side with no fence. The biggest challenge at this time was hiding the surveillance vehicle so that our female investigator could secure a protected view point in the public perimeter trees and obtain videotape from that location.

Gloria established surveillance on foot in the forest at the rear of the property. Within thirty minutes of commencing surveillance, the back door of the house opened and two large boxer type dogs rushed out into the yard and commenced patrolling the property. Hiding behind a tree and keeping absolutely motionless, she waited for the dogs to settle down. The dogs were soon joined by a male and the dogs became focused on that individual. Getting the lay of the land, our investigator departed the area.

The second day of surveillance Gloria elected to conduct surveillance by herself as I had received a criminal investigation file from a client working that particular Saturday.

Heading out on the job at around 5:45 a.m. she attended at the property and, upon arrival noticed several additional vehicles parked in the driveway and noted several biker clad males drinking beer on the front porch of the residence.

Returning to the position in the forest at the rear of the residence, she set up her camera and commenced surveillance. Hearing activity at the front of the property, our investigator repositioned to the treed area on the west side of the property and noticed that the males had gone into the house.

At around 10:30 a.m. four males exited the house and sat around drinking beer on the front porch. Although it was early for drinking beer, it was possible that they had been drinking all night as they were loud, raucous, laughing and telling jokes. Among the four males sitting on the porch, our investigator noticed a small, slim built male, bearing a strong resemblance to the claimant - as described by our client exit the front door and sit on the steps at the front of the porch.

Using field binoculars, our investigator was able to identify the claimant by the prosthetic arm attached at the left elbow. There was a strap around the prosthesis and the entire assembly went over the shoulder and hooked around the upper chest. He was a nice looking young man with an infectious smile and it was easy to take a liking to him as our job is to observe, report and present the facts.

Several hours of drinking beer ended with all four males departing in their vehicles and, upon leaving the property, calling out the name of "Kevin" as they left; further establishing that the claimant was in fact the subject of our surveillance. After his friends had gone, the claimant returned into the house.

A short time later, having repositioned to the rear of the residence our investigator observed the claimant come out the back door, walk down the steps and retrieve a step ladder from outside the garden shed. He dragged the stepladder over to a fruit tree and leaned the ladder against the tree. The subject went back to garden shed and returned with a long handled pruning saw and began pruning the lower branches of the tree. The claimant then undid the leather strap on his prosthesis, shook the prosthetic arm off his elbow and, climbed up the ladder, used the pruning saw to reach the upper branches.

The claimant did a thorough job of pruning the entire tree and, stepping back to the ground; he gathered the branches into a wheelbarrow and removed them to the side of the house.

It was evident that the claimant was quite strong and able to hold tools while assisting with the upper portion of his disabled arm and negotiating around the fruit tree.

On the third and final day of surveillance, the claimant came out on the porch around mid-morning and after ten minutes of reading went into the house and let the dogs out in the back yard. The dogs were barking loudly in the direction of our investigator and the claimant asked: "Who's out there, boys?" the dogs pinged on Gloria, hiding in the tree line about fifty feet from the house. With a woof and a snort, one of the boxer dogs raced towards the gate of the property. Gloria grabbed her equipment and fled the area without touching the ground! By the grace of God, our tenacious investigator managed to outrun the two dogs.

Videotape established that the claimant was indeed capable, to a limited degree, of using his prosthesis for picking up objects and performing certain other functions. Notwithstanding his valiant efforts at recovery and adaptation, the claimant was severally disabled by the accidental loss of a portion of his left arm.

CHAPTER 26

Surveillance Case #7

This particular case is one that my wife will never forget as a result of a surveillance file that took place in a remote community in a rural area.

Being assigned approximately 30 hours of surveillance on a bodily injury claimant, Gloria proceeded to locate the claimant as the client did not have a recent address. Quite often insurance claimants move and/or give a different address, like a friend or family member to the insurance adjustor in an attempt to evade observation. And, on occasion, it has been known that the client's legal representatives will warn the client of the possibility of surveillance.

In the early morning on a dry September day, she proceeded to the address found through a location search and commenced surveillance on a large house with several outbuildings. The acreage was located in a rural farming area. The first indication that something was amiss was the silver foil on the barn windows, which was not far from the main house. In addition, there were heavy power lines and water hoses connected to the barn and, the flow of human traffic from the house to the barn was frequent. It was possible that a "grow op" was the farm's means of income. The area between an adjacent gravel road and the large barn was littered with abandoned vehicles.

The house was about 150 feet from the edge of the property and sloped upwards and away from the front wire fence. Simply stated, the windows of the surveillance van were lower that the front door and windows of the residence.

Quite often we use different surveillance vehicles to minimize detection while working on difficult files. In this case, our investigator was using our white 1989 Volkswagen Westphalia Vanagon, that had tinted windows and curtains all around the inside of the windows; including a curtain across the rear portion behind the front seats so that anyone looking in the windshield would only see a curtain in the seemingly dark interior. It was an ideal setup and generally worked well for surveillance. There was a fridge, sink and air vent on the roof for hot days.

Acquiring considerable videotape for the first two days and thinking that it was time to get out of the area and, while filming out through a side window curtain, our investigator noticed a large male, dressed in full biker gear strolling towards the barn in the company of two other males. As will sometimes happen, the slight movement of the van curtain alerted the large male to her presence.

Loping toward the van, the large, irate and intimidating male climbed the fence and proceeded to try every door on the van. Thankfully all the doors were locked as is our protocol. The male then jumped up and down on the front bumper of our vehicle and hollered: "I know you're in there!" He then ran back into the farm yard.

Gloria crawled into the front seat of the vehicle and quickly departed the area; as the keys are always left in the ignition of the locked vehicle for just such situations. Looking alternately in both side mirrors she noticed the determined and daunting biker pursuing her in a bright yellow Trans Am.

In desperation my wife called for my advice regarding the pursuit. Unfortunately, I was engaged in a meeting with a bereaved family in my capacity as a lay pastor, as their mother had passed away several days earlier. In the middle of going over the Celebration of Life program, my cell, which was lying on the table beside me, rang.

Out of compassion for the bereaved family, I ignored the ringing phone. On the next call seconds later, I glanced at the phone and saw that it was my wife. Excusing myself from the family meeting, I answered the phone and reminded Gloria that I was engaged with the family and would call her back a bit later. My wife started telling me in an agitated voice that she was being pursued in the surveillance vehicle by an angry biker thug in a yellow Trans Am in a remote area miles from the Trans-Canada Highway. Not totally understanding the gravity of the situation, I reminded my intelligent and resourceful spouse that I was unable to assist her at that moment as I was consoling the grieving family. As everyone can imagine, the next move that I made was to push the "end" button on the cell phone.

It would take me a long time to fully assuage the feelings of my wife and, for ignoring that moment of her trauma. However, I made a huge error in judgment by hanging up the phone and turning back to the awestruck family who had been listening to my overly anxious wife. Several minutes later, I received a third call from Gloria, who wanted to know what to do in that particular situation. Without thinking, I suggested that she drive to the nearest police station. Of course, she hung up and I heard nothing else for the next twenty minutes.

Sometime later, I learned that my brave and resourceful wife spotted a corner gas station and quickly pulled into the pumps, opened her driver side door as if to exit the vehicle and watched while the large biker thug unfolded himself from the Trans Am, which had parked immediately behind her vehicle. Once the biker was fully upright and stepping away from his muscle car, Gloria slammed the door of the Westphalia and quickly sped out of the gas station, taking the first left secondary road and listening as the rumbling Trans Am sped down the main road. She had successfully eluded her pursuer. After waiting for approximately half an hour to make sure the coast was clear, she proceeded to the nearest RCMP detachment.

Unfortunately again, I was not there to deal with the situation and, the not too sympathetic male police officer wanted to know if she had been threatened; in spite of the large male biker jumping on the van, screaming, raging and affecting a high speed pursuit into the gas station, the constable deemed those actions to be insufficient reasonable and probable grounds for the police to open a file. As an aside, this rarely happens with the police, as most law enforcement officers appreciate the tireless efforts of private investigators and consider us part of the legal community.

The following day we collectively agreed to change vehicles and double up on surveillance. This was achieved by having one vehicle positioned on the road behind subject's property and the other vehicle further up the road in an inconspicuous place. This proved to work well and when the claimant came outside our investigator was able to observe his activities from the rear of the property; as we had learned earlier that activities at the rear of the property had been of concern to the client.

After two more days of clandestine surveillance, we were able to obtain sufficient evidence to conclude the file and establish that the claimant was in fact involved in illegal activity and that the claimant exhibited no physical limitations in his activities. It was not the last time that our investigator encountered dangerous situations while conducting Sub Rosa activities on angry and dangerous biker males.

CHAPTER 27

Surveillance Case #8
The Watch Cow

This surveillance file relates to a law firm client whose large firm represents a significantly large number of insurance companies in the defence of bodily injury files. We conducted hundreds of files for this client as we were known as the husband and wife team. In fact, we received many telephone calls over the years from insurance adjustors all across Canada asking, without preamble "Is this the investigation company of the husband and wife team?" Our delighted response was always "Yes" as the files were mostly high quantum claims requiring two investigators.

Being assigned this particular out of town file meant a holiday within a job; as it was also a well-known fact by our clients that we regularly used either our Westphalia van or small travel trailer for remote jobs on and off Vancouver Island. In this case, the assignment was on one of the outlying islands in a remote village in the Johnstone Straits.

Packing up our gear and readying ourselves for an adventure within our work schedule, we set off for the ferry dock, arriving at the Gulf Island where the surveillance was required. Shortly after arriving in the remote community we located and confirmed the address of the claimant, found a suitable surveillance position and commenced a minimum of three days of observation.

The claimant in this particular file was an artist who had recently moved from New York and purchased a three acre oceanfront hobby farm at the very far end of the small island. The roadway approaching the claimant's farm house had a fenced field parallel to the house and offered very little place to park our surveillance van.

Affecting a reconnaissance along the beach front on foot located an ideal surveillance position under the boughs of a huge old growth cedar tree on the roadway across from the claimant's property. In fact, there were other bushes and trees nearby which enhanced our cover approximately seventy feet from the driveway of her home.

The majestic sweeping branches of our surveillance tree covered the entire ground near the base of the tree so that the boughs came out about six feet from the trunk, affording us complete obscurity. Sneaking in behind the tree and nesting in under the boughs, we believed that we were not visible to anyone and set up our gear.

Within thirty minutes of commencing observation, and thoroughly enjoying the beautiful breeze from the ocean, we maintained scrutiny on the house and adjoining buildings. Like all surveillance jobs, it is important to be aware of a 360 degree radius as people strolling along a road somehow manage to ping on something not quite in keeping with nature. However, in this case, people were walking past our position as we remained undetected.

What we did not know was that the claimant had a yearling bovine in the field in front of the house and that the baby bull had recently been weaned from his mother. Sensing something amiss in his neighbourhood; the mommy-sick baby bull slowly ambled over to the far end of the field which happened to be close to the tree we were under.

After a few snorts and a lot of bawling, the annoying bull began tossing his head from the ground up while bawling and pointing his nose toward our position; like an elephant bellowing and swinging his trunk forward, in an attempt to alert his mistress to the fact that there was someone hiding under the cedar tree.

Without any warning, the claimant, an

attractive middle-aged woman, dressed in gardening attire exited the side door of the farm house and walked over to the agitated animal. Simultaneously, an elderly couple walking along the road in our direction stopped and looked at the bawling beast that was "maawing" and shaking his head towards our tree.

Videotaping the claimant climbing up on the fence in an effort to appease the agitated bull, the elderly couple commenced telling the claimant that something was bothering the animal and that she should find out what was ailing him.

To our relief, the claimant sweetly told the concerned couple that the baby bull was missing his mother and was just trying to tell the whole world about his misfortune. For the next 15 minutes we obtained sufficient videotape to establish that the clamant was more agile than she had reported to the insurance company.

After completing the assignment two days later and, while being subjected to the ranting of the hyper-vigilant baby bull, we ceased surveillance with enough evidence to conclude the file. What is most interesting about this particular file is that we are not permitted to edit evidentiary video or audio tapes and, if required, we would be compelled to attend court and testify to the authenticity of the evidence. In this particularly humorous case, the three days of surveillance evidence, approximately ten hours of actual videotape, was punctuated by the bawling bull which greatly amused our client. In retrospect, the claimant should have paid more attention to the tenacity of the vigilant "watch cow."

CHAPTER 28

Surveillance Case #9
The Rambling Handyman

Surveillance is one of the most interesting activities that the majority of people would like to undertake, although few people are ever in a position to obtain a security licence to legally observe their fellow man. The reason most people who exhibit a propensity for intrigue, find watching people without being seen appealing, is that human nature is generally quite predictable and observing from a covert position how other humans interact, communicate, and respond to intrinsic and extrinsic situations is highly entertaining. How other people live is also a source of entertainment. People commonly say to us when they learn that we are private investigators: "Oh, I would be good at that". The following case acutely describes the eccentricities of human nature:

This case is about a middle-aged overweight single male who had a history of more than 21 motor vehicle accident claims during the three year period preceding our assignment to conduct surveillance on him as a result of motor vehicle accident number 22.

The subject barely moved, while lumbering around in his one-ton pick-up truck with an open wooden wired box frame around the flat deck: filled with shovels, rakes, hoes, garden tools - standing erect in two large plastic garbage cans. The truck and driver could be seen and heard from blocks away as the vehicle swayed from side to side while negotiating turns, stops and mall visits to collect bottles, cans and grocery carts for a 25 cent return fee. He was short, heavy and slow; but a real character in the community.

His latest claim was a two vehicle, low impact MVA and the financial exposure to the insurance company was not that high, although he had received compensation for more than 21 minor motor vehicle accidents over a short period of time. Getting videotape or photographs of his activities was relatively easy; however, he barely moved so there was very little incriminating evidence against him.

For weeks we followed this interesting character as he and his older vehicle lumbered and rattled around the city. If by chance we lost him in heavy traffic, it was only a matter of stopping, parking and listening for the crashing sound of tools, rakes and shovels clanking in the box of his truck. In addition, after raking a lawn, which generally took several hours as he barely moved – step by step, he would walk back to his work truck and stand the rake, shovel, corn broom or whatever tools he had at that time, upright in a plastic garbage can. He was indeed hilarious to watch.

On the final day of surveillance, our investigator observed the claimant using a heavy-duty rototiller in his entire backyard. What a surprise! He must have thought that he was completely unobserved.

After several weeks of observing the unkempt middle-aged male, one could not help growing fond of this eccentric individual who laboriously engaged himself in a multitude of seemingly meaningless activities. He was either in excruciating pain or just an adept *confidence man* who had learned how to manipulate the system.

Years after finishing the claim, we would see him crashing around the city in his vintage truck not realizing that the surveillance was over. Or, maybe he was just working on another claim - his only apparent means of existence. Law firms, insurance companies and mediators were continually looking for the multi-claim bodily injury man. He had indeed perfected the BI (bodily injury) claim process.

CHAPTER 29

Fire Investigation #4

Over the years, our company was assigned a variety of different types of investigations, as we are trained in all aspects of investigating. On the other extreme, requests for background information, locations; employee honesty and cash register thefts were not uncommon. In the case of the fire in the basement of a well-established English Style pub on the north of Vancouver Island, I was called by an insurance company adjuster who asked me to meet with the owner of the pub. The adjuster provided contact numbers and the details of the claim.

Arriving at the establishment at approximately 9:00 a.m. on a pre-arranged meeting with the pub owner, I was provided immediate access to the basement area where a washing machine and clothes dryer were sitting in a corner behind a partial wall. Fire damage to the basement was significant and flames had progressed into the floor joints, burning into the bar area above. Damage was extensive but contained to the north side of the basement and upper portion of the lounge area.

Conducting a cursory inspection of all the fire damage, I zeroed in on the clothes dryer as it appeared to be the origin of the fire. The dryer door was open and the top, sides and front of the dryer were buckled, charred and nearly destroyed by the fire. Looking up at the basement ceiling, it was evident that the fire had progressed from the dryer to the pony wall across from the dryer and ignited the 4 x 4 floor support posts and progressed upwards and into the basement ceiling, where the fire load had then burned upwards into the bar. The damage was not structural; however, the estimated water and fire damage to the building was significant. The insurance claim would certainly cover loss of earnings, repair and restoration to the basement, bar lounge and resultant loss of furniture and equipment.

One of the due diligence requirements for establishments with commercial insurance policies is to confirm an occupancy licence and, in this case a liquor licence, in order to establish that the insurance policy was in fact covering a licenced operational business. Many insurance claims are denied due to the fact that the establishment is not in compliance with government and local regulations. Checking with the applicable municipal office is part of that process.

After viewing the damage inside the building, I proceeded outside and conducted a thorough inspection of the perimeter of the building, property lines and adjacent structures. Searching the legal title of the property is also mandatory for a fire loss and loss of business income to be established.

After obtaining photographs of the exterior of the building, I proceeded to the local volunteer fire department, identified myself and requested that the on-call dispatcher page the fire chief to call me at the station. Fortunately the fire chief, who is also the Local Fire Commissioner (LFC) was close by and immediately came into the fire hall.

Learning that I was a certified member of CAFI (Canadian Association of Fire Investigators); preliminary protocol was dispensed with and we got down to the basics of the fire call at the pub. The chief confirmed that there was no structural damage to the basement or upper lounge floor and, after overhauling the fire, called the owner and upon her arrival, handed the fire scene over to her.

Generally, the fire department does not leave the scene until security is put in place, something that my company was licenced to do, in addition to my credentials to investigate the fire. Often, the volunteer fire departments will not call security without the approval of the insurance company, or the municipality, as the expense of security could become an issue if the fire claim is denied for reasons like material change of liability. However, in this case the fire chief advised me that the building maintained integrity and had been boarded up, and security was not necessary as the owner had taken responsibility for the property.

The chief established from the call out log that the fire call had come into the station at approximately 2:30 a.m. from a passing motorist who saw the smoke coming out of the north side of the building at ground level, which I knew to be the exterior wall where the dryer vent was located. The chief also told me that upon arrival at the fire scene, one of the fire crew members pulled the hydro meter, which is mandatory for all structural fires, thereby shutting down the electrical load to the building. The hydro meter is retained by the fire department and handed over to B.C. Hydro at a later date. Gaining access through the front door, the fire fighters overhauled the fire within an hour of entering the building, which greatly reduced fire and water damage to the structure and did not require mutual aid from neighbouring fire departments.

Securing the scene, the fire chief said that the owner had no idea how the fire had started and told him that they would contact their insurance company first thing in the morning.

Returning to the pub, I again met with the building owner who was gathering some documents together for my report. Obtaining photographs, videotape and a witness statement from the owner, I asked her to provide me a copy of the staff work schedule two days prior to the fire and, the day of the fire. The owner made a phone call to the bartender who had been on shift the night of the fire and directed that the female employee come into the pub as soon as possible.

When the female bartender arrived, I requested a private room to interview her about her movements on the evening prior to the fire starting. During this meeting, I learned about the recent painting of the basement which the owner had forgotten to mention to me in our interview earlier. I did not find this suspicious as the owner appeared overwhelmed by the fire and had been under the impression that the clothes dryer had been burned in the fire and did not know the cause of the fire.

The bartender explained that she knew nothing about how the fire had started and told me how she had secured the bar for her next day shift: stocking the bar cooler, cleaning the bar counter, replenishing the beer kegs, pop dispensing machine, washing the bar floor and checking out the bathrooms.

While taking her statement, she

remembered that she had an occasion to go down into the basement for some cleaning supplies and, reaching the bottom of the basement stairs, found three or four wet rags on the floor. Thinking that they were dirty bar rags that had been tossed down the stairs by one of the bar staff, she took them over to the dryer, opened the door and threw the rags into the dryer and pushed the button on the machine to dry the rags and went back upstairs. Forgetting about the rags in the dryer, she finished her closing routine, set the security alarm and left the building. She thought that the time was around 2:00 a.m. After taking a statement from the employee, I returned downstairs.

Having now learned about the paint rags on the basement floor, I commenced taking the clothes dryer apart which proved to be beneficial to the investigation, as I found charred fragments of cloth in the back floor of the dryer drum. Scooping out the shards, I sniffed the scraps of cloth and it was evident that there was a faint odor of Varsol paint thinner, even though the rags had been mostly destroyed by fire. Laying all the electrical components of the dryer on a piece of white tarp, which was in my fire investigators kit, I took photographs of the dryer cord, plug, wiring harness, relay armature and electrical connectors to the element. Nothing was charred or indicated that the fire had been caused from an electrical arc fault. In fact, the dryer had been fully operational at the time of ignition, which occurred inside the dryer drum when the heat from the dryer caused the paint rags to catch fire. To further confirm this hypothesis, I located the multi-breaker box, and locating the 240 amp switch for the washer and dryer, shone a flashlight on the breaker switch and did not find any soot smudges on the inside of the breaker switch which clearly ruled out an electrical arc fault. Photographs of the breaker panel and switch were obtained to establish and document those facts.

Going back upstairs, I advised the owner that my investigation was complete and, in my opinion the fire had been accidental and that a report to the insurance company would be submitted within 24 hours.

CHAPTER 30

Fire Investigation #5

One of our major insurance company clients who we had maintained an excellent relationship with for more than 20 years, called our office late on a Friday afternoon advising that a claim had just been opened on the total fire loss of a floating restaurant in the Clayquot Sound area of Vancouver Island. The details of the claim were being faxed to our office that afternoon and they enquired if I would be able to leave immediately for the area.

As a result of the remoteness of the place where the restaurant had been located, travel to the area would take a full day plus a ferry to the inlet where the floating structure had been moored prior to the fire. Photographs of the restaurant prior to the fire would be in the package being sent by facsimile.

Gathering the fire investigation gear and loading the truck, I set out on the 167 kilometre trip to the small remote village of Tofino, at around 4:30 a.m. the following morning. I knew the investigation would take a minimum of four days and prepared myself accordingly. Arriving in the District of Tofino, in the Clayquot Sound, which is part of the Pacific Rim National Park Reserve, I checked into a motel around 6:00 p.m. Saturday evening and made arrangements to attend at the local RCMP detachment that evening.

The District of Tofino has a population of just over 1,900 residents and was named by the locals around 1904, as it was situated in the Tofino Inlet. The name Tofino was derived from the Spanish Rear Admiral *Vincente Tofina de San Miguel,* a cartographer and explorer, who sailed into the inlet in 1792. The local records show that Tofino was incorporated in 1932, with the official opening of the local post office.

The Ahousaht Band is a First Nations government reserve whose principle settlement is on Flores Island, a small Island in the Clayquot Sound off the west coast of British Columbia and is accessible only by water taxi or boat. The Ahousaht First Nations indigenous people are a part of the Nuu-chah-nult Nation and are known for their care of the land and exceptional fishing skills. Flores Island is northwest of Tofino and is accessed by boat through the channel past Vargas Island with several small islands in between.

Attending with the RCMP watch commander, it was learned that very little was known about the fire as the floating restaurant had been in the Barkley Sound area which required a water taxi trip out to the inlet where the floating building had been moored. In addition, by the time the police had arrived at the fire scene the following day, the structure had been completely destroyed.

Detailing my assignment to the police, I asked if police divers had been dispatched to the last known position of the restaurant and, if not, how much notice would the dive commander require getting on site. Surprisingly, the police divers would be available the following day and I was provided a contact name for the dive officer.

Many years earlier I had been trained as a ships diver while serving in the Royal Canadian Navy and knew the routine well.

The following morning, I took the water taxi from Tofino village to the remote cove across from Flores Island where the floating building had burned to the waterline and sunk.

Several hours later, I stepped ashore at the remote village across the Sound from the Ahousaht First Nations Reserve on Flores Island (a National Park) and, the first thing that I noticed was a large wharf jutting out into the bay and four huge pilings about two hundred feet from the main dock. Walking out to the end of the dock, I noticed that the pilings were now separate from the former floating restaurant as the dock attaching the float house to the main wharf no longer existed. The four pilings were charred and burned at the waterline.

Going over to the general store, I asked where the federal wharfinger was located. A wharfinger is the person responsible for the custody of goods, leasing, renting or management of a federal wharf and the securing or lease of any house boats or buildings attached to the wharf. The counterperson in the store told me that the wharfinger was currently off somewhere in the village and provided me a phone number where he could be reached.

Several minutes later, I made contact with the wharfinger and we agreed to meet for lunch at the local eatery. Meeting the wharfinger was an absolute delight. He was a former yachtsman and had sailed boats of every length, type and sail. We hit it off immediately and, over lunch he told me that the floating restaurant had been secured to the main wharf for about two years. He described the building as a humongous cedar covered monstrosity erected on a barge with a gangplank access to the main dock. The building had a fresh water and shore power connection to the wharf. He further went on to say that about two months ago he had issued a removal order to the owner to tow the restaurant out of the harbour within 30 days, as the owner was not in compliance with the regulations for mooring. He remonstrated that the owner left for a period of two weeks, came back, was concerned where to move the floating building and told the wharfinger that he had nowhere to moor the restaurant and asked for an extension of time to tow the floating building out of the Sound.

Finally, the deadline arrived and the building had not been moved. Having been issued one last directive, the owner hired a barge tug and towed the restaurant out into the harbour and secured the restaurant to some pilings.

After about a month of being tied up in the bay, the local regional district sent the owner a registered letter and directed that the restaurant had to be moved within 48 hours from the pilings, or he would be fined and charged a service fee for the removal. Apparently, most of the community was aware of the order to move the restaurant, which might have prompted someone to take action on their own initiative.

The wharfinger suggested that I speak with the young man working on his boat at the end of the wharf, as he knew how to get in touch with one of the former employees of the restaurant. Meeting with the young man working on the wharf, he was most cooperative with providing details of the restaurant management, moorage, employees and the fire.

The witness told me that the owner had hired several employees to help run the restaurant which operated during the summer months. He recalled seeing one of the employees and the owner talking on the wharf and overhearing the young man tell his boss that he was quitting his job and moving away from the area. The contact gave me the name and phone number of the employee who was now living in the north of Vancouver Island. Before finishing with the witness, I asked him if there was anything else that he could recall.

After a moment of silence, he stated that he had heard that a fisherman from the First Nation Reserve on Flores Island was sitting at a campfire on the beach at around 3:00 a.m. and, while stoking his campfire heard a loud bang, followed by a flash of light and moments later the restaurant was totally engulfed with flames that brightened the dark night sky. According to the witness, the fisherman jumped in his tin boat, raced out to the burning restaurant and sped around the building until it finally sank in about 50 feet of water.

The last question that I asked the witness was if he knew the name of the fisherman. His response was no; however, everyone on the Reserve knew him because he camped on the beach most nights. Just as I was leaving to find a boat to get over to the Reserve, the young man offered to take me there when he finished with his work on the Wharf.

Going back to the general store, I again located the wharfinger and asked if he knew anything about the fire and he related the same story about the fisherman racing around the burning restaurant before the barge, building and everything on the deck of the barge sank. He did not know a name; however, he said he would be easy to find and I took a statement from him regarding the order to move the restaurant from the main wharf and, eventually from the pilings in the bay. After finishing his statement, I asked if I could get a copy of the letter that he had sent to the owner to remove the restaurant, prior to the fire.

Returning to the wharf renewed with energy from the chase, I met with the witness and he took me over to the beach where the fisherman had seen the floating restaurant catch fire.

Within a few minutes I located the fisherman and, after interviewing him, learned that he had in fact seen the owner's boat tied up at the restaurant around 6:00 p.m. the night of the fire, and recalled hearing the boat leave before dark. I obtained a statement of what he had seen, as the statement was exactly how the incident had been described by the first witness.

Returning to the main wharf, the place where the restaurant was initially tied up and then later tied to the pilings across the bay, I took photographs of the entire area. Armed with the witness statements, I hired a water taxi and returned to the Tofino motel and made a phone call to the former employee of the restaurant.

Our initial introduction on the phone did not provide forthcoming information on the part of the former employee. Although he appeared evasive and had nothing to say about the fire he provided a good description of the restaurant construction.

He told me that the entire building was decorated inside with cedar shakes and wooden furniture and the outside was covered from roof to barge with cedar shakes. I again asked for clarification about the inside walls and he re-iterated that the walls of the restaurant were covered from ceiling to floor with cedar shingles inclusive of driftwood logs around the bar and wooden driftwood tables.

When I switched the interrogation to the details of the relationship between himself and his employer, he said that the owner was a well-liked person and that as far as he knew; the restaurant had to relocate from the wharf because of some new mooring regulations. I asked him if he had heard any rumours about who might have caused the fire and his response was that anyone could have taken a boat over to the restaurant and lit the fire. I thanked him for his cooperation and told him that he would most likely receive a call from the police.

The next morning, I was contacted by the RCMP dive team who advised that they would be leaving the Tofino Wharf at 9:00 a.m. the next morning and that they would meet me on the wharf before departing for the cove where the fire occurred.

The following morning, the dive team took me to the cove near Mears Island across from the Ahousaht Reserve and, after a twenty-five minute dive, the team surfaced and one of the divers flashed the international sign of thumb and round forefinger symbol signifying "found it", as they swam back to the wharf. On the wharf and shedding their diving gear, the senior member advised me that they had located an airtight wood burning stove on the sea bed, a 30 pound propane tank and an exploded aerosol can inside the metal stove.

Several hours later, the heavy metal stove was hauled to the surface and placed on a small barge, with the aerosol can and other debris that had been found not far from the pilings where the restaurant had been secured before the explosion and resultant fire.

Bringing the barge over to the main wharf we began going through the debris. Taking pictures of the metal stove (with the door open), exploded aerosol can and the propane tank, it was easy to reconstruct how the arsonist had laid a cedar and hard wood fire in the airtight stove, thrown an aerosol can into the open door of the stove, opened the propane tank valve and exited the restaurant and left the scene.

The evidence supported that when the aerosol can reached a significant temperature, the can exploded showering sparks and burning wood into the propane saturated room; creating an explosion that ignited the cedar shingled walls and wooden furniture inside the restaurant. The amount of fuel source in the room greatly enhanced fire progression thereby spreading to the exterior walls of the building which further added to the fuel load. It was estimated that within minutes, the exterior siding of dry wooden shingles erupted into flames and the entire structure was gone in a matter of minutes. The explosion from the propane tank and resultant inferno of the crackling cedar shingles is most likely what the fisherman heard from the Ahousaht Reserve. In the case of a suspicious fire it is very difficult to prove any wrongdoing on the part of the claimant. The burden of proof is very clear there must be motive, opportunity and a direct physical link to the fire scene.

To our understanding, the owner was nowhere near the area at the time that the fire had broken out and, anyone with a preconceived notion could have gotten onto the restaurant barge, opened the propane tank, thrown an aerosol can into the airtight stove, lit the fire and sped away in a boat. As far as I know, no one was ever charged with the burning of the floating restaurant.

The only observation that was made on my report about the cause of the fire was a comment about the fisherman who had been seen racing around the moored restaurant; several minutes after the fire was noticed from the wharf across from the moorage. We leave those conclusions to the insurance experts who approve and distribute the funds as required by the claimant's fire insurance policy.

CHAPTER 31

Suspicious Death Case #1
The Florida Scam

In June of 2001, I received a telephone call from a young woman in Ontario who told me that a friend of hers on Vancouver Island had recommended me as a private investigator, and asked if I would be willing to assist her with a strange situation. Taking notes, she told me that over the past few days she had been receiving phone calls from a telephone number in a place called New Port Richey, Florida and that when she answered the phone no one was there. After several more calls to her home, she finally called the number and a female voice asked her to leave a message.

Asking the prospective client if she knew anyone in Florida, she replied that she thought her estranged brother who she had not heard from in over 15 years, had at one time lived in Florida. In addition, she thought that maybe her biological father, whom she did not know, might have been trying to call her and had not left a message. Being a manager in the federal government, she was reluctant to make contact with anyone in Florida.

Taking the file and obtaining as much information as possible, I made arrangements to fly to Tampa Bay Airport which is not far from New Port Richey, located in Pascoe County a suburb of Tampa – St. Petersburg counties located off Highway I-19. As a matter of interest, years earlier I had been in Key West Florida with the Canadian Navy while transiting a Canadian Navy Destroyer from Halifax, Nova Scotia via the Panama Canal and up the west coast of North America to Esquimalt, British Columbia.

Arriving in Tampa Bay, I rented a vehicle and made my way to a local motel in New Port Richey. After checking into the motel, I called the phone number provided by my client whereby a female answered the phone and identified the place as a mobile home park. I identified myself as a private investigator. What is interesting about the United States and, the fact that I am a Certified International Investigator, is that most American private detectives are permitted to carry hand guns and the general public treats them with preferred respect. Also, in Canada, private investigators are not permitted to refer to themselves as detectives. When I learned that the contact was the manager of a mobile home park, I made arrangements to meet her at the park office first thing in the morning. As it was late in the evening I stayed in the motel for the rest of the night.

At approximately 8:00 a.m. the following morning, I attended at the park office and met a pleasant middle-aged woman named Sarah who told me that there had been an older male residing in Unit # 25 in a converted trailer that he had set up years earlier. When I asked about the male, whom she identified as Cliff, she told me that he had been found dead in his trailer and the Dade County Sherriff's Department were looking for next of kin to identify the body, as they suspected he had been murdered in the trailer.

Sarah also said that Cliff's black Ford pick-up truck seemed to have disappeared since the body was removed by the coroner. She went on to say that she had found a telephone number of a woman who lived in Ottawa, Canada and had called her twice, but hung up both times not wanting to be the one to advise her that her father had been found murdered.

Wanting to get started with my day, I asked the woman to take me to the trailer and, when we arrived at the unit, the manager extracted a key from her pocket and opened the door. When I asked her about how she came to have access to the trailer, she explained that Cliff trusted her to have access as he was a long distance trucker and sometimes was gone for weeks and wanted her to check on the place when he was away. In support of that statement, Sarah told me that she had not seen Cliff or the black truck for several weeks and, while checking on his place, she discovered his partially naked body slumped over the toilet. Running out of the trailer, she called the police.

She seemed credible, as she had told me earlier that she was married, her husband was disabled and that out of compassion for the less fortunate people in the trailer park, she took care of the elderly people who lived there. As she was giving me the key to the trailer, I asked if she knew who the police detective was that she had spoken with on the day she found his body. Sarah gave me the name and phone number of the detective.

After a brief search inside the trailer, I located a shoebox in a cupboard above the fridge and, lifting the box down, found over 25 identification cards and credit cards in just as many names. The dead man's name at the time of death was Clifford Allen Presley and his date of birth was shown as December 17th, 1938. Going through the documents, I noted that for every identification card there were two or three gas and credit cards in those names. The deceased man was indeed an enigma. The strange part was that the man's vehicle, a black 1996 Ford pick-up truck was nowhere to be found. I made a note to ask about the vehicle at the police station later that day.

Going through the add-on room, a 12 by 15 foot wood constructed bedroom combination living room suite, I located another box in a cupboard above the wood stove which produced a bank book at the First National Bank in New Port Richey, complete with a safety deposit box key and a Last Will and Testament in the name of Daniel Richard LaBrie, born in Camrose, Alberta. The copy of the Will named three beneficiaries who were listed as living in Canada and a life insurance policy in the amount of three hundred thousand US dollars. Each of his three children was named and the amount for each child was indicated as one hundred thousand dollars. Not recognizing the surname, I called my client and she confirmed that they were in fact the beneficiaries named in the Will, although their surnames had changed and that her sister was also living in Ottawa, Ontario while her estranged brother was living somewhere in Florida. Going through the second box, I found bank statements, dividend cheque stubs and a safety deposit box enrollment form.

Locking up the trailer, I proceeded to the Dade County Sheriff's Department where I had the good fortune to meet with the detective who had attended at the trailer when the body was discovered slumped over the bathroom toilet.

Producing my international investigator's credentials and Canadian PI's Licence, I was ushered into the detective's office where I was told that the Dade Sherriff's Department had suspected that the male had been murdered from the injury on the side of his head and the way he was slumped over the toilet.

After pronouncing the male dead, the corner had the unidentified male transported to Mountain Heights Funeral Parlor in Dade County. The detectives' name was Bill, and by looking at my PI and C.I.I. Licence, Bill noted that we were the same age. We instantly became friends and I was grateful when he opened his files and began sharing vital information. Looking at the photograph of the deceased man revealed that he was about six feet tall and weighed over 450 pounds. After the autopsy, the coroner's office confirmed the COD (Cause of Death) as the onset of a major heart attack while sleeping on the floor in the add-on room.

The suspected time line was that he woke up feeling pain in his chest, vomited on the floor before rushing to the bathroom in the trailer attached to the add-on and upon reaching the toilet, the victim fell onto the toilet bowl, striking his head on the edge of the toilet bowl rim, at which time he succumbed to a heart attack.

While speaking with Bill, I pulled out my investigators note book and gave him the name of the deceased as per his Last Will and Testament and, the 21 aliases found in the trailer. Running the birth certificate name confirmed that he was in fact Daniel Richard LaBrie from Alberta, Canada. Upon learning his birth name, Bill told me that I needed to attend at the coroner's office later in the day and positively identify the deceased from the photograph on his driver's licence as I had the authority from my client to represent the family.

Before leaving the Sherriff's office, I asked Bill to run the third beneficiary's name through the computer and, we positively identified a male born the same day as the deceased's youngest son who we discovered was incarcerated in a federal correctional facility in Florida under an alias surname. Leaving the Sherriff's office, I went over to the deceased's bank located in New Port Richey and produced Clifford Allen's Presley's identification card and after providing my credentials, made an appointment to open the safety deposit box with the branch manager the following afternoon.

Arriving back at the trailer, I called the deceased's employer and informed them that Clifford Allen Presley had passed away from a coronary infarction and that I represented his daughter and her two siblings, and had a notarized letter from his daughter, one of the beneficiaries, authorizing me to accept payment of the life insurance policy. I also advised the employer that I would fax the Certificate of Death later that afternoon after I met with the coroner. The employer agreed and directed that I fax all the relevant documents to their head office in Tallahassee, Florida.

While I was sitting at the deceased's kitchen table going over legal documents that required faxing to the trucking company, a rental car pulled into the driveway and a middle-aged male knocked on the door. Opening the door, the male walked in the trailer and identified himself as the deceased man's half-brother from Canada.

Demanding proof of Identification, the male provided a Canadian passport and British Columbia driver's licence. In addition, the male produced a business card stating that he was a self-employed Certified General Accountant working in Surrey, British Columbia.

While the half-brother was wandering around the trailer opening and closing doors and cupboards, he spoke quickly in a hyper, non-stop manner about how close he had been to his half-brother "Rocky" as he referred to his sibling and, the fact that he had just seen his brother, in this very trailer and that the last time that he had been to see his brother, the brother changed his Last Will and Testament and named him as full beneficiary in trust for the three adult children. I suspected he was high on something and being disturbed by this sudden change of plans, I asked to see a copy of the recent Last Will and Testament. Producing a hand-written copy, I had nothing to compare the handwriting with as I required a minimum of ten specimen signatures to confirm authenticity of handwriting.

As a fraud examiner in addition to other qualifications, I told the half-brother that before he could be provided any information about his deceased half-brother, he would need to provide photocopies of his Canadian passport, Driver's Licence and any other photo Identification that he had on his person. He became agitated and told me that he was the legal beneficiary and that he had promised his half-brother "Rocky" that he would make certain that his three estranged children would be given their inheritance. In musing over his non-stop verbiage, I did not recall seeing an identification card with the name "Rocky" in the box of ID Cards.

Guiding the alleged half-brother out the door of the trailer, I locked the door and walked over to the trailer park manager's office and requested three copies of each of the documents. Returning to the trailer, where the male was standing on the porch, I told the half-brother that he was required to identify his sibling at the funeral home. Providing him the address, he departed in a huff.

After the alleged half-brother left, I called the British Columbia Association of Certified General Accounts in Vancouver, British Columbia and provided them the name of the male who's ID and passport I had copied. After providing all the information, they advised that they would call me back within the hour. Two hours later, I called them again and was advised that the half-brother was no longer in good standing as a CGA as he had been charged and convicted for cocaine use and defrauding his clients.

Upon confirming what I had suspected, I Immediately called the bank to inform them that the deceased's half-brother was not authorized to access his bank accounts and, the bank manager advised me that he had just left after withdrawing all the funds and cleaning out the safety deposit box. In addition, she volunteered that the half-brother was on his way to Tallahassee to collect his inheritance, as the bank called the employer on his behalf and established that he was in fact the beneficiary and that I was not authorized to receive the money. I asked to speak with the bank attorney and was provided a female attorney's name and phone number. Unfortunately, when the female attorney returned my call she said that there was nothing the bank could do and that the matter was closed.

Knowing that the fraudulent relative was on his way to Tallahassee, I called their Head Office and was told that there was nothing that could be done on this day as the office closed in ten minutes and that the legal officer for the company would call me in the morning.

Calling the Dade County Sherriff's Office and connecting with Bill, I quickly brought him up to speed on the half-brother's actions at the bank and the fact that he was on his way to collect the life insurance money in Tallahassee. Before hanging up the phone, I told Bill that Cederick LaBrie, the half-brother, had told me that he was flying to Manila in the Philippines to marry his sweetheart - before going back to Vancouver. In addition, I told Bill that I had demanded a copy of his passport and British Columbia Driver's Licence when he was at the trailer. Bill was ecstatic and said that the Dade Country Sherriff's Office would try and arrest him at the airport the next day if I would swear an *Information* of the details of the fraud. After hanging up with the detective, I drove over to the Sherriff's Office, swore an affidavit and gave the detective a copy of coloured photocopies of the passport and Driver's Licence.

The following day I proceeded to the federal institution where the third beneficiary was incarcerated and upon showing my credentials was permitted into the prison to speak with Daniel LaBrie's son. Sitting with him in a private visitor's room, I told him that his father had been found dead in his trailer. He was not surprised, as he had only just recently, for the first in his life before being sentenced to five years, met his biological father at his trailer and had no desire to have a relationship with him for what he had done to his mother. When asked about his father's pick-up truck, he told me that one of his friends had borrowed the truck before his father had passed away. Feeling sorry for the boy, I made arrangements to rent out the trailer and divide the rental money between the three beneficiaries as a monthly payment from a trust account opened at a bank in New Port Richey. The young man was very pleased as he had no money in his prison canteen account.

Returning to the motel just before midnight, I made a note to see the trailer park manager in the morning about changing the locks on the trailer and offering to pay her fifty dollars a month if she would rent the trailer and deposit the money into a trust account that I was going to open the following morning.

Later the next morning, I spoke with Sarah at the trailer park who stated that she was pleased to rent the trailer, collect the rent and deposit the monies into the trust account for the three beneficiaries.

Calling the client in Ottawa, she was brought up to speed about the lost inheritance, the trailer rental agreement and that she and each of her siblings would receive approximately $330.00 USD a month from the trust account and, that the local authorities were trying to locate the half-brother who had absconded with the money and locate the black pick-up truck. In conclusion, the drug addicted half-brother was never heard from again and we suspect that he is somewhere in Asia living with his 28-year-old bride.

.

CHAPTER 32

File Intake Preparation

Before proceeding into the next segment, I am going to share the basics of client intake, case preparation and file management. Administrative functions are not the most romantic part of private investigations; however, those functions are absolutely vital in assuring that file management and report preparation are handled with diligence and that written reports are accurate, clear and factual.

During the period 1990 to 2011 inclusive, we had the honour and pleasure to be retained by three highly respected lawyers who through their dedication and love of the law, were appointed as judges in the province of British Columbia. The first lawyer, Ivar Bruhaug was appointed as a Provincial court judge in Prince George, on May 3rd, 1973 before retiring from the Bench to reopen his practice again in Victoria; the second lawyer, Richard Goepel, QC of the Vancouver firm of Goepel & Watson was appointed a Supreme court judge in Vancouver, on October 1st, 2001 and later appointed as Justice of the Supreme Court of Appeals on November 7th, 2013 and; the third lawyer, Adrian Brooks, QC of Brooks & Marshall in Victoria, was appointed judge of the Provincial court of British Columbia on March 17th, 2009. Those three former clients were the crème de la crème of jurists.

Speaking of exceptional lawyers, I would be remiss if I did not share the amazing abilities, professional experience and personal qualities of lawyer, G.E. (Ted) Beaubier, principle of Beaubier Law, whose practice is in Nanaimo, British Columbia. I had the honour of meeting Ted Beaubier during an insurance investigation in the Nanaimo area in 1992 that led me to the local court house seeking information on the claimant. While searching court records, I came across a court document naming Ted Beaubier as the Crown Prosecutor who had recently and successfully convicted the subject of my enquiries during his ten year tenure with the Crown Prosecutors office. In private practice, Mr. Beaubier has proven himself to be a solicitor of impeccable character while displaying kindness and humour in his diligent pursuit of justice. He is very well respected in the legal community and it is an honour and pleasure to be working with Ted.

Attending unannounced at his general practice office later that day and, meeting Ted and his dynamic legal secretary Janet Povey;

we established a working relationship that has spanned more that twenty-seven years. In fact, in July 2017, through our ongoing professional relationship, I joined his firm as the first licenced private investigator to be hired as an In-House Investigator. Another benefit of working with Ted was that when I joined his firm, I was already a Commissioner for Oaths and Affidavits for the Province of British Columbia: resultant of my tenure as a Veteran's Advocate.

Getting back on topic, I vividly recall being trained in file management, evidence preparation, and the recording and reporting of crucial facts resultant of investigative inquiries.

As the well-known sign on the office wall says: "No job is finished, until the paperwork is done" and, those words were taken to heart by our team of investigators. Keeping investigators note books neat, well organized and chronological in order of the facts is paramount – since the documents might be required for future scrutiny.

For example, when I was employed as a Veterans Advocate between 2011 and 2014, I had the occasion to ask an RCMP client if he still had his patrol notebooks available as I believed that they would be instrumental in proving his disability appeal which, in fact did happen, and he consequently won his appeal based on evidence from the time of his injury while on duty.

Keeping the case file neat and organized with date, time, and persons interviewed and what was said is crucial; as neat, accurate, clear notes and documented evidence are what makes the difference in establishing the truth and supporting the evidence.

Videotape and photographic evidence can also prove crucial in any trial or mediation. If the evidence is suspect, has been tampered with or has not established the chain of custody then the evidence has no legal value.

While training under-supervision investigators and, at the end of a particularly long and stressful day of surveillance, pursuit and vehicle leap frogging (two investigators in separate vehicles front and back of the target on a hyper-vigilant subject), the paper work at the end of the day was one of the most important requirements of the assignment. In that regard, I can't recall how many times trainee investigators would try and justify their messy and unorganized files while stopping the vehicle, grabbing the camera and stomping on the file to get into position in the rear of the surveillance vehicle. The excuses ranged from: "I was busy, the file is not important, don't worry about the footprint on the cover, I got the job done, right?"

The response was that investigative files are evidence and must be preserved at any expense. Sloppy or suspect evidence can taint a case in minutes. So, learning it right the first time will stay with an investigator for the duration of their career and even after retirement. Thousands of cases, of every type, unequivocally hone the investigator into a formidable opponent or ally.

Doing five or six different files in any given day is mind boggling, even to the most experienced investigator. However, for the first three years of starting my investigations company that is just what was required. I could never see the sense of heading out on an assignment at 6:00 a.m. with only one file. What happens when the subject fails to appear? Well - put the file at the bottom of the pile, open the next one and go to work. Those professional work habits are the difference between a successful investigator and a onetime client. Quality with quantity works in that regard.

Another important professional trait is to never leave the office without a full gas tank, snacks, water, spare pens, film, binoculars, charged batteries and a road map. Being prepared is crucial, as sitting at the curb looking for the subject – after they left ten minutes before you arrived, is a waste of your client's time. Good work ethics created unimpeachable evidence which ultimately kept our investigations company in business.

CHAPTER 33

Bar Surveillance #1
The Eye is Quicker than the Hand

Over the years, my wife and I were occasionally hired to conduct bar or pub surveillance as a result of the establishment losing money behind the bar or on the floor. Being non-drinkers certainly did not create a useful blind; however, sitting at the bar and chatting up the bartender, who was generally the subject of our investigation - was never difficult.

In this particular case, the owner of the bar, grill and lounge was losing exorbitant amounts of money on the busiest days of the week: days when the establishment had been selling two and three thousand dollars a day in beer, wine and liquor. Hiring us to watch the till, bartenders and the servers always proved to be a challenge, as the place was generally noisy from servers ordering, the patrons, band music and activity at the bar.

On the first night of surveillance, we noticed that the hyper-vigilant and ostentatiously distracting female bartender was taking the opportunity to leave the till open when she appeared to be busy. When the activity quietened down, the bartender had a pile of cash sitting on the open till drawer. The hand being quicker than the eye, the drawer closed and the bartender's hands were down at her sides. This continued the entire night and, during one of her infrequent breaks, she went out the fire escape door on the pretext of having a cigarette, at which time I went out the front door, walked around the building and observed the attractive bartender handing hundreds of dollars to a male that I had not seen before. The bartender looked distraught, anxious and full of guilt and remorse. This activity went on for the next two days and, on the Monday morning while meeting with the client, he expostulated that his till was short over $1,300 since Thursday night.

During the client meeting, the owner was advised that his senior female bartender was skimming from the till when the establishment was busiest and, that just before closing, when everyone was listening to the last few songs of the band, the bartender was meeting a male in the alley behind the bar and handing him a stack of cash: bills taken during her shift. To say the least he was livid. However, I suggested that he not dismiss the bartender until I had the opportunity to conduct an investigation on the male who was taking the money from the bartender. This was suggested for two reasons. The first being that the establishment was a union shop and the second was that a wrongful dismissal would cost him additional loses through union arbitration.

The plan of action was to find out who the male was and then request a union meeting with the employee, owner and union representative and, at that meeting, present the evidence of what the bartender was doing and supported by affidavit evidence from my partner and myself, offer the employee the opportunity to make restitution and resign from her position – or else her accomplice would also be charged with theft. Our client agreed and he made arrangements for a meeting with the employee and her union representative.

A few days later, my partner and I attended the meeting with the owner, employee and union representative. The smug look on the employee and union rep's faces did not last long when I opened the meeting. Without preamble, I spoke directly to the union representative, who I knew would not defend a thief who was also a member of his union: because unions do not like losing cases as it weakens their control over the business.

Looking directly at the union representative, I told him that my partner and I were licenced investigators and while watching the female bartender working on Thursday, Friday and Saturday nights, we observed the bartender skimming money from the cash register. Before he could respond, I raised my hand and suggested that he listen carefully to the rest of the evidence. With a glare that could melt ice, the union rep closed his mouth and my next sentenced started out with, "And we know who her accomplice is and his name. So, the next step is charging the employee and her drug trafficking boyfriend with grand larceny; which will most likely bring jail time for the boyfriend and probation for the employee!"

Anticipating the first words from the union rep, I again held up both hands - palms up waiting for his response to the evidence. His question was: "What do you want?" Those were the words I was anticipating and, looking at our client, he nodded his head for me to continue.

My demand was: "The establishment owner is petitioning for full restitution, resignation of the employee and a sanction from the union. If restitution is not made within 48 hours, our evidence will be submitted to the police. The employee's boyfriend, who is on parole at this time, will be arrested and sent back to jail." I then added: "However, we can't guarantee he won't be arrested as the offences are criminal in nature"

The union rep looked at his client, stood up and invited her into the hallway. Ten minutes later the employee and union rep returned to the room and with a pained look on her face the employee agreed to the two conditions. The pub owner asked for the agreement to be in writing so that the money could be paid back within 48 hours. As the employee immediately made restitution and resigned from the establishment, there was no need to contact the authorities.

CHAPTER 34

Surveillance Case #10

During a busy time when our company had approximately 16 files on our desk, a well-established insurance company from Vancouver and, a new client, retained our firm to investigate and, if necessary, conduct surveillance on a young woman from the lower mainland who had been involved in a serious motor vehicle accident resulting in a bodily injury (BI) claim. As in most BI cases, the more medical information provided, the less work is required on the file.

In this particular case, the claimant provided a written statement to the insurance adjustor claiming that she was unable to work in her position as a bartender in a very large and busy bar in Vancouver. The exposure to the insurance company was significant and, the client relocated to Vancouver Island to convalesce from her soft tissue injuries.

Performing a background investigation on the client, an attractive, vibrant young woman with impeccable work ethics, revealed little about her present physical condition and the ability to work in her chosen profession. Locating the claimant at her new address, our female investigator commenced surveillance. We knew from the client's report, that the claimant had been injured in a relatively new and expense bright red coloured Trans Am which had been a total write-off in the motor vehicle accident. Although we did not know what the claimant was currently driving, human nature generally reveals people to be creatures of habit and, we discovered that the claimant was in fact driving a bright red muscle car, albeit not as new as the one that was written-off in the accident; however, it was a good start to the surveillance operation.

For the first two days of observation, the client was inactive and was only seen briefly outside while walking to and from her vehicle. However, on day three, the day that we usually like to wrap up surveillance, the client exited her residence early in the morning carrying a large blue binder. Departing the residence, our surveillance investigator commenced pursuit and observation.

Over the next six hours, the claimant drove her vehicle to over 15 small businesses in the community where she was residing. At every stop, which was frequent, the claimant took the large blue binder into the place of business and remained inside for approximately 20 to 30 minutes. By the end of the first day, our investigator had videotaped all the activity in addition to creating detailed notes of the name and address of the business; adding the phone number after researching through the phone directory. At the end of the day, the claimant proceeded back to her residence, parked her vehicle and went inside. During the investigation, we learned that the claimant was a single mother and wanted to be home for her child's after school care.

The following morning, the claimant left her residence early with a cardboard box and the large blue binder and affected the same pattern of visiting businesses that day. It was difficult surveillance as the claimant stopped and parked her vehicle without much warning to the pursuing investigator and, finding a parking spot nearby presented a challenge. However, information on the business was diarized and videotape obtained. Again, as per the previous day, the claimant continued several hours of attending at various business places, carrying the box and binder into the business and returning to her vehicle within 20 to 30 minutes. It was tiring keeping up with the active young woman. At the end of the day, the claimant returned home and our investigator ceased surveillance.

On the third and final day of surveillance, a crucial day in the ability of the claimant to work three consecutive days, the claimant maintained the same energetic activity from nine o'clock in the morning until three o'clock p.m. Upon returning home at the end of the busy day, the claimant parked her vehicle and went into the residence. Wanting to establish that the claimant was in for the night, our investigator remained on surveillance well past dark.

Providing a verbal report to the client the following morning, we were directed to attend with all the businesses that the claimant had visited over the past three days and obtain a statement from each business as to the nature of the claimant's activity. That evening, our investigator prepared a full page chart of the route taken by the claimant in her pursuit of clients and, a pattern emerged whereby the claimant was deemed to be selling advertising in a coupon book to the businesses she had been attending. This was further established when our investigator made a pretext phone call to one of those businesses enquiring about their advertising needs. The pleasant owner stated that she had just signed on with a young woman who was working as an advertising agent for a local marketing company. Expressing disappointment, our investigator asked the name of the marketing company. Having obtained that vitally important information, our investigator ended the conversation.

Wanting to establish that the claimant was working on the fourth day, our investigator attended at the residence and maintained surveillance. Within 15 minutes of watching the claimant's residence, the attractive, limber and, apparently happy claimant exited her residence and headed out to more local businesses in the community. After spending the entire fourth day working, the claimant returned home at the end of the day and our investigator ceased surveillance.

The following day, our investigator commenced a routine of phoning the new business clients of the claimant and requested an interview with the person responsible for signing up for the coupon marketing advertising. Attending at over 30 businesses, we established that not all of the businesses had subscribed to the claimants advertising program. Those were the businesses that our investigator concentrated on as we did not wish to cause any harm to the claimant as the work was not physically demanding although the new sales position would significantly reduce the claimant's wage loss quantum, a benefit to the insurance company.

After interviewing all the businesses where the claimant was unable to sign them up as customers, we presented our report, videotape and witness statements to the client. One thing that is important is that to the credit of the claimant, she admitted, on the advice of her attorney, that she had in fact started working for the marketing company and was actively soliciting clients in her new job. This pleased our female investigator and she could tell from surveillance observations that the claimant was attempting to mitigate her losses and was in fact unable to work in a bar while standing on her feet all day. The claimant's honesty was indeed refreshing and we think of that industrious young woman whenever we drive past one of those businesses.

CHAPTER 35

Surveillance Case #11

In the spring of 1995, while operating our business out of a small store front office space in Langford, B.C., and late on a Friday afternoon, I was sitting at my desk finishing up some paperwork for the weekend. The good thing about this particular Friday was that for the first weekend in months, my wife and I were getting a weekend off from our company. In fact, we had made plans to go boating up island and take in some sunshine.

Nearly finished for the day, the front door of the office opened and an agitated young man, around 30 years of age strode into my office and blurted out that he was being followed by somebody and needed to hire a private investigator. Rising from my desk and closing my office door because there were confidential files on my desk, I gently guided the male to the front office and sat down on the couch, inviting him to take a seat.

He was about six feet tall, strong looking and well-built with a head of shocking blonde hair flying all over the place. He was wearing soiled blue jeans, jean shirt and jean jacket. His clothes appeared to be soiled from actual soil, as if he were a farmer of some sort. Looking out the window of my office, I noted that he was driving a dirty blue jeep, also covered in dust and soil. I memorized his licence plate in case he was in my office on a pretext.

Refusing to sit down, the prospective client paced around the room in obvious distress. He spoke with disjointed statements and his thoughts were random and rambling. I immediately recognized his fear and, possible drug induced rambling. Over the next hour, the young man related, in juxtaposing fashion that: "These people are trying to steal my business and I need help in proving what they are doing."

Every time that I attempted to ask a question, he interrupted me and began the entire litany of fear and paranoia all over again. Finally, he sat down on a chair and began sobbing with his head in his hands. Feeling immense empathy for the young man, I asked him to slowly and calmly start from the beginning.

Over the next several hours, which by this time was nearly 5:30 p.m. he related a questionable and bizarre story about how his father had recently passed away and left him a well-established and profitable farming business on the north island and that his sister was trying to take the business away from him as she claimed, in court documents that he was incapable of operating and managing the business. He further went on to say that every night, while watching television in the large farm house, strange things were happening: flashing blue lights bouncing off the walls after dark, wire probes coming out of electrical sockets and strange and eerie noises coming from outside the house. Crashing and banging noises in the barn and all manner of frightening alien activity.

While he was ranting about what was happening to him on the property, he pulled out a large wad of cash and threw it on the table in front of me. I asked him what he was doing and he responded that there was a $1,000 on the table as a retainer for me to attend at his remote farm and conduct surveillance on the property.

Agreeing to take on the case, a file was opened and we obtained all the necessary information to start the job and before taking the money from the table, I clarified: "I will only take on this case if you agree to accept the findings of my investigation and, carry out all the instructions of my recommendations." Agreeing he provided an address and departed the office.

Arriving home, my wife and I prepared our surveillance van for a weekend of surveillance activities and, within the hour headed out on a four hour drive north. After securing an RV parking spot for the weekend and a late dinner in the area of the client's farm, we set up our Westphalia surveillance van (with fridge, stove and water in the unit) and commenced surveillance in the dark, alongside a row of evergreen trees that allowed us full vision of the house, driveway and barn.

Upon commencing observation on the large and stately property, we noted blue flashes coming from the upper room of the house, which we believed was a T.V. room. In addition, we did not see the client's jeep in the yard and assumed that the vehicle was parked in the large barn. During the night, we shared four hours of surveillance each and, there being nothing out of the ordinary left the farm at daylight.

Returning the following evening, now being Saturday night, we set up our surveillance position and commenced observation on the house, barn and property. Again, we noticed the blue flash coming from the upper room. The only eerie sound that we heard was the forlorn hooting of an owl in the nearby trees. Leaving at dawn, we went back to the RV park where we were sleeping during the day.

That evening, being Sunday night, we again set up surveillance and, at around 2:00 a.m. while the T.V. was flashing blue light in the upstairs room, the client's jeep drove into the yard and parked at the front of the residence and several minutes later the client went into the house. Observing the house until dawn, we departed.

After checking out of the R.V. park, I called the client on the telephone and told him that we had finished three nights of surveillance and that I needed to meet with him and detail our report. He agreed to see me later that afternoon.

Attending at his property a few hours later and, at the client's request, I conducted an entire sweep of the residence to establish that there were no listening devices, probes or hidden cameras in the house. Briefing him on the 24 hours of surveillance and the results of our observations, I presented him a written invoice for travel, mileage, RV park expenses and, hourly wages for the three days of activity.

Without hesitation, the client paid me the balance of our invoice and, as delicately as possible I reminded him of the agreement that he had made with me on Friday afternoon at my office. As I had earlier reported that we had seen nothing suspicious on the three nights, I told him that I suspected that he was addicted to cocaine and that the weird and strange things he was seeing and hearing were as a result of cocaine psychosis and, furthermore, that he needed to check himself into a detox centre and get treatment for his addiction.

Waiting for an onslaught of denial and his demanding a refund of his money, the client looked up and, with tears streaming down his face reached out and shook my hand and agreed to seek immediate treatment. Before leaving, I told him that I was knowledgeable in addiction treatment from my former work with police services, and wrote down a phone number and contact at the Victoria Life Enrichment Society.

Twenty years later, while sitting in a barbershop chair in Duncan, a clean cut, well dressed male with short blonde hair entered the shop and looked at me sitting in the chair and, in front of about six people said in a loud voice: "are you Ace, the private investigator that saved my life in 1995?" I looked directly at him and said:

"Yes, I remember you well and always wondered what had happened to you."

With a huge smile on his face, he grabbed my hand from under the barber's cape, shook it vigorously and while looking all around the room said: "I followed your advice, went into treatment, kept my farm and have never felt better in my life. Thank you Ace and God bless you!"

While tears obscured my vision, I watched as the former client turned and walked out of the barbershop. No pun intended; however, the high that I felt that day was the pinnacle of the many years of helping people in my profession as a private investigator. The question will always be: what is the balance of probability that I would meet that man again – some 20 years later and, in my hometown?

CHAPTER 36

Civil Investigation Case #5

Many years after helping the young farmer with his addiction problem, I received a phone call from a well-spoken First Nations man that was very disturbed about the physical and emotional state of his wife and three children. He told me that he would prefer meeting me in person as he did not trust telephone lines. Looking at the telephone display on my office phone before taking the call, I noticed a phone prefix for a remote northern area on Vancouver Island.

Before I could ask where he lived, the male, who spoke with impeccable grammar, said that he was in my area and asked if he could come to my office. I explained that I was not in my office as I had call-forwarded our office phone but could meet him there in 15 minutes. Providing the address, I went to the office; prepared an intake file and he arrived as promised.

Meeting the 30 something year old male, his wife and children, he proceeded to disclose, in a detailed manner, that his three children were six, four and one years old and that he and his wife operated a small grocery store out of their home located on a remote First Nations Reserve. He claimed that his neighbours were discriminating against him because he was successful and described that behaviour as the *crab syndrome*, because when a strong crab is on the verge of crawling out of the barrel, the other crabs pull them back down. As the children were in the next room it was suggested that his wife take the children for a walk while he provided the reason for wanting to hire my services.

After his wife left, he told me that his two young children: the four-year-old and the one-year-old had been sexually molested by two local police officers, health care workers and a neighbour. He further believed that the police and Family and Children's Ministry were discriminating against him as they had threatened to remove their children from the home. He presented himself as articulate and well-educated and I found the story quite concerning.

Opening a file, I cautioned him that he needed to stop lamenting all the evils that were going on in his life and allow me the opportunity to investigate some of the disconcerting allegations. He reluctantly agreed and we made arrangements to attend at his home, a ten hour drive from my office. Without prompting, he produced a thousand dollars cash retainer and large envelope filled with police reports, doctor examinations, government records and school reports.

After the client left the office, I started working on the file. Something that I had not mentioned to the client was that I knew the Sergeant NCO i/c of the remote detachment in his community, by virtue of the fact that his brother had been a military policeman that I knew from the police school in Borden, Ontario. I was having a hard time believing that the police were involved in the abuse of the children and their family.

The client had said some very damaging things about some of the local professionals. One of those stories was about a police vehicle stopping his wife with the youngest child in the vehicle and arresting his wife for impaired driving. During that arrest the children had been apprehended by a police woman and taken to the RCMP detachment. The accusation was that the female police officer had molested the one-year-old child and that my client had proof from a highly regarded child obstetrician that the one-year-old boy had been sexually assaulted.

The following week, while driving into the northern town, attending at the police station and producing my PI Licence, I advised the sergeant that I was working on a private matter in the area. There was no need to tell the detachment about my client as the file was confidential; however, I knew from years of experience representing First Nation clients that it was professional courtesy to inform the band council that I was going to be investigating on Reserve Land. This is always a difficult thing to do, as the Reserve is noted for vigilance, and any stranger is viewed in a suspicious light.

Attending at the band office, I provided my name and received permission to come and go on the Reserve and after spending an hour with my client at his store, I headed back to the main village to secure a motel for the night. Just as I was leaving the Reserve, a First Nations RCMP police car stopped me on the very edge of the highway exiting the Reserve. A male First Nations constable, whom I recognized from the detachment earlier, with full wig wag lights flashing approached my vehicle and ordered me out onto the road. He had his hand on his service weapon and rudely turned me around and pushed me up against my vehicle. Turning around I asked him the question that annoys most police officers: "Excuse me Officer, what are your reasonable and probable grounds to stop and detain me?"

With a sneer on his face, he let go of my arms and as I turned around to face him, he demanded my driver's licence and credentials. I replied that he had already seen my credentials at the detachment a few hours ago, as he had photocopied them and that he had no grounds to harass me. His response was that it was protocol to obtain permission to come onto a Reserve and that he was arresting me for trespassing. In response to his threat, I told him that I had attended at the band office earlier, checked in with the band administrator and that he was wrong in his assumption. His response to that salvo was: "Prove it" Reaching into my sports jacket pocket; I pulled out the business card of the band administrator. He was visibly annoyed and told me that I had five minutes to leave and never come back.

Now, his directive that I leave the area and not return, really raised my hackles and suspicions that the officer might be complicit in the abuse of my client and his family. In fact, his threats were contrary to the permission given to me by the NCO I/C of the detachment. Turning away from the constable I got back into my vehicle and drove away.

Heading north into the village, I returned to my motel and phoned two witnesses whose names had been given to me by the client during our meeting earlier that day. One of the witnesses was a Caucasian lady who lived about a mile from the motel.

After phoning her and identifying who I was, she agreed that I could come to her apartment at that time. Within minutes I was at her apartment and after going into the unit, she locked the door, closed all the curtains and told me that we needed to whisper as walls have ears. The woman was scared, nervous and visibly shaken by my visit. Calming her down and explaining that I was a "good guy", she told me that three of the local police officers were into cocaine dealing and that one of them was a female officer who had been observed molesting the client's children.

After hearing the witness relate the despicable events that she had personally seen, and learning about the threats made against her - by the same male officer who had tried to arrest me earlier that day, I obtained a sworn statement. Before leaving the apartment, the witness volunteered that she was leaving the community as she feared for her life. Obtaining a promise from her that she would keep in touch with me and, armed with two more witness names, I left the apartment. Returning to my vehicle, I realized that the investigation was beginning to concern me regarding the suggested police corruption and the motive surrounding accusations about drug dealing police officers. It was hard to fathom and I sincerely believed that the sergeant, whose brother I personally knew, could have no knowledge of what these particular First Nation constables were doing.

Hunting down the two other witnesses proved a difficult task, as by the time I left the apartment, paranoia was rampant in the community and I was being shadowed by First Nation police vehicles. Not to be intimidated, I attempted to obtain two additional independent witness statements; however, no one was willing to speak with me about the client's children.

Returning to the Reserve, I attended at the client's house and briefed him on what had happened to me after I went to the band office. His response was that the entire tribe hated him and his wife, because of the accusations he had made about his children being molested.

While I was questioning him in more detail as to the complaints, he told me that not only were his children being abused and ostracized in the community, but that his wife was constantly being stopped by the Native police and being arrested for impaired driving and possession of cocaine. In addition, the client produced a medical report from a well-known and highly respected child sexual assault specialist from Victoria who had written a full report, which I read at that time, establishing that the one-year-old baby exhibited signs of being sexually abused. It was devastating and I asked for a copy of the report. Unfortunately, the client was beginning to question my motives and this caused me concern as I was there in the best interests of the children. Calming his fears, I told him that I would absolutely take the evidence out of the community and deal with the evidence at a higher level. He seemed mollified and told me to stay away from the police detachment as they were all corrupt.

As I was outside getting into my vehicle a male from across the street walked over to me and started berating me for listening to the lies of my client. He was becoming aggressive and I started back into the client's house.

As I was about to enter the house, a police cruiser raced around the corner with all lights flashing, and a male and female Native constable exited the vehicle and told me to raise my hands and stand against the building. I reluctantly complied and the client locked his door with me standing alone outside.

After being frisked and, for the third time in two days, told to produce my credentials, the female constable ordered me to get in my car; as the police were going to escort me off the Reserve. As I was getting into my vehicle, I memorized the name tags on their uniforms.

Driving out of the Reserve, several miles beneath the speed limit, and reaching the main highway south, I looked into the rear-view mirror and noticed that the police vehicle was still following me and stayed with me until I was approximately 15 miles south of the village.

Looking back a last time, I saw the First Nations police vehicle execute a u-turn and head back towards the village.

To say the very least, I was annoyed and now certain that unlawful activity was being perpetrated by the First Nations officers and that the three of them were definitely exhibiting guilty knowledge and mistakenly assuming that they could intimidate me into abandoning my client, closing the file and never returning. On my way south, I stopped at a restaurant and devised a plan of how I was going to expose the corruption of the First Nations officers and the abuse of the client's children.

On the way through a major hub city on the Island Highway, I drove into the mid-Island RCMP Island Headquarters detachment and asked to speak with the senior officer, who happened to be an inspector with Internal Affairs. Getting an audience with the inspector established that he had just come back from Ottawa and was aware of systemic abuse of Native children in remote areas; especially in communities of the north island.

Opening my files for the officer and sharing that I knew the brother of the NCO I/C of the detachment and that I believed him to be unaware of the crimes, I provided the inspector copies of all my notes, obtained his business card and headed south. It is remarkable that the offenders' attempts to drive me away had led me directly to the Criminal Investigation section of their organization. What was also notable was that the inspector had just returned from a briefing in Ottawa directly related to the theme of my concerns and complaint.

After arriving back at our company office, I called a retired judge friend who was now practicing law again in the capital city and made an appointment to discuss the case. The following day, I met with the lawyer and after briefing him on the status of the file, he called my client. In a three-way telephone conversation with my client we agreed that the lawyer would represent him and his family and that both of us would attend on the Reserve the following day.

Returning to the area late the following night, we checked into a motel and summoned the client to a meeting in our motel room.

An hour later my client arrived and was taken on as a client of the law firm. After obtaining a retainer and signing a client contract, the lawyer and I left the motel with the intention of obtaining sworn depositions from the three witnesses.

By the end of the day, we had obtained sworn depositions from all three witnesses. Returning home, the lawyer instructed me to continue inquires with the RCMP Internal Affairs inspector and report those findings when finished.

Several days later, the lawyer phoned me and told me that he had just received a telephone call from the client who ranted and raved for about 15 minutes that he did not trust either of us and had accused us both of being in a conspiracy with the police, children's ministry and the doctor who had examined the children.

The lawyer then told me that the case was over and that we should close our files. I had known the former judge for many years and absolutely respected his legal opinion; as my wife and I had done dozens of files for his law firm.

Several weeks later, I received a call from the Internal Affairs inspector who told me that the male constable who had harassed me on the Reserve had been arrested and was no longer employed with the RCMP. I asked about the other two members and he advised that they were still under investigation. At that time, I told him our file was closed.

About three months later, I received a telephone call from the former client whereas he proceed to tell me that the police were arresting him for public mischief and that he was going to name me as an accomplice of the corrupt police department. My response was that he was to never call my office again.

Unfortunately, while in a mid-Island retail store with my wife, we observed a male slinking around inside the men's clothing section and, looking in that direction noticed the former client intently staring at us. Making eye contact with me, he rushed over and started accusing me of stalking and harassing him. It was at that time that I first suspected that he was under the influence of a narcotic or opioid, and that he appeared to be suffering from paranoia.

It was very sad and my heart went out to the children. We will never know whether he was stressed out and self-medicating as a result of the trauma of his children, or if he was using drugs at the time that he hired my services. The positive outcome of my investigation was that the First Nations constable was charged, found guilty and sentenced by the court.

CHAPTER 37

Fire Scene Investigation #6

My involvement with this fire scene was by pure coincidence when I met the homeowner on the street and he explained that a fire in the family home was being delayed payment from the insurance company based on a report from the local fire department that the cause of the fire appeared suspicious. Of course, the claimant did not know that the insurance company was obligated by law to pay the insurance claim; once the claimant had signed a proof of loss: as evidence of arson is not sufficient in itself to deny payment of the insured's claim.

Not knowing this, the claimant asked if I knew a good private fire investigator who would be willing to take a look at his house which had been nearly destroyed by fire. Feeling quite sorry for the local business man, I gave him my business card and suggested that he contract my services to take a look at the fire scene in an attempt to clear up any confusion, and communicate my findings to the insurance company. He appeared pleased and went on his way.

Several days later, he phoned my office and asked for assistance. I agreed and attended at the local fire department and started gathering information about the fire. The fire department was very cooperative and told me that the municipal fire investigator and the General Investigative Section of the RCMP were in fact investigating the fire.

Contacting the municipal fire investigator, I informed him that the homeowner had hired my services to take an independent look at the cause of the fire." No problem" said the municipal fire investigator, "Take a look". Before hanging up the phone, I asked my contact if he knew of any reason why the insurance company had denied the claim. His response was that he had discovered accelerant splash marks on the kitchen cupboard doors and the homeowner was unable to explain the presence of the marks, which the fire department had reported to the insurance company. As I knew the insurance company quite well, I called their office and explained that the homeowner was desirous of clearing up the matter and moving on with the settlement. The adjuster was fine with me taking a second look.

That afternoon, I attended at the fire scene with the RCMP GIS (General

Investigative Section) officer and went through the house room by room, noticing the accelerant splash marks on several kitchen cupboards. It was most evident that someone had stood back from the lower cupboard doors and splashed a petroleum-based fuel on the doors. The way this is done, is that the individual takes a gas, kerosene or diesel container, stands back four or five feet and shakes the container in a back and forth motion while soaking the flammable material with an accelerant. This in itself is not proof that the homeowner started the fire. Rather, it merely indicates that someone splashed the doors.

Another indication of low burning accelerants is a phenomenon referred to as spalling: the rapid expansion of concrete from an accelerant being poured on a concrete floor and being ignited. For years, the scientific belief was that the rainbow sheen on the burned concrete floor was indicative of spalling; however, this concept was dispelled and discredited as being an indication of arson; as a plastic container of lawn mower gas sitting on the concrete floor could just as easily been the cause of the fire.

Having spoken with the homeowner a few days earlier, he advised me that he was out of town on the day of the fire and that his wife had been staying with a relative at the time of the fire. I explained this to the police officer, who was not a certified or trained fire investigator, whereby he agreed with my statement. As we walked around the house, I noticed two important details that had not been reported in the initial report from the fire department. The first detail was that there were no female clothes in the master bedroom closet and the second detail was that it was a known fact that the homeowner's wife owned a bird. The bird cage was missing from the living room and the bird survived the fire. The officer left the scene and nothing more was said about the birdcage and lack of women's clothing in the master bedroom.

Speaking to the homeowner later that evening, I asked him if he and his wife were getting along and, if not, what were the details of that conflict. He reluctantly admitted that his wife was no longer interested in living on the remote acreage as she wanted to sell the house and move into the city. He also explained that their teenage children wanted to live closer to town.

Returning to the municipal office, I again spoke with the fire investigator who had initially attended at the fire scene upon the request of the fire chief. Explaining my observations regarding the bird cage and lack of women's clothing in the nearly destroyed bedroom closet, the investigator pointed out that the wooden hangers could have been destroyed in the fire. Getting his attention, I declared that there was no evidence of any charred or burned clothes on the partially burned closet floor and elaborated on the fact that the bird cage was missing from the living room. In addition, I pointed out that a woman would remove her clothing and take the bird out of the house if she had intended to start the fire. He was now convinced and stated that he would speak to the RCMP.

In speaking with the client, he was advised that it was evident that his estranged wife had either started the fire or hired someone else to torch the house. He did not seem surprised and I never heard from him again. The disposition of the claim was not brought to my attention and, I did not charge a fee for my services.

CHAPTER 38

Fire Scene Investigation #7

Having investigated approximately 50 major fire scenes in addition to many smaller ones between 2001 and 2011, I recall that the most impressive fire investigation was that of a large home situated on a lake in a remote community on Vancouver Island. This particular fire scene was one for the fire investigators manual and has been used as a training aid by fire marshals and insurance investigators all over British Columbia.

It was late September, which is generally the busiest time for the fire departments after the summer weather moves south. The cause of most September residential fires is the rekindling of fireplaces and woodstoves which have been shut down for the summer.

Homeowners often forget to clean the chimney and burn off the creosote in the airtight or wood burning stoves, which quite often results in a fire in the first few weeks of the fall. In addition, in the case of an arsonist who burns down his business or house for financial gain, a

September fire is less suspicious, as firebugs know this is the best time to either hire "Teddy the Torch" or undertake the job themselves. Just for the record, this investigator has seen many attempts at arson by those ignorant criminals who think they can get away with anything.

Fortunately, fire scientology is so far advanced from 30 years ago that it is virtually impossible for anyone to light the perfect fire, as every molecule in natural or man-made fibres has an ignition point, flash point and burning rate.

In this hilarious anecdote, the homeowner was broke, deep in debt and obviously wanted to get out of his mortgage. The home was a single family dwelling built near the beach on a large lake in a remote area. The three foot crawl space was above ground and the double doors of the crawl space could be opened to accommodate a breeze from the lake on warm summer days.

As a point of interest and, as explained before, fire departments are not mandated to contact insurance companies when there is a fire loss. However, the police are notified if the fire is suspicious or if there are injuries or death. In the case of this fire, the local fire commissioner contacted the police due to the suspicious nature of the fire. The police then contacted the homeowner and directed him to provide a statement regarding the origin of the fire. Most guilty fire bugs call their insurance company hoping that an independent investigation will render causations as arson by unknown persons. The homeowner did indeed call the insurance company and they in turn contracted me to investigate the fire of which they knew no details of the cause.

Attending at the remote fire scene, I noticed that the fire had been set deliberately as the breeze ventilation doors under the floor in the above ground crawl space were wide open and the entire crawl space was filled with partially charred timbers, dried tree branches, driftwood, old rubber tires, wads of rumpled newspaper and a noticeable smell of an accelerant. There was so much debris under the house that there was not enough space to oxygenate the fuel load.

It was beyond understanding how the fire progressed to a heavy smoke stage before being extinguished by the local volunteer fire department. The chance of the fire progressing to chemical reaction stage was next to impossible.

Crawling around on my hands and knees at the perimeter of the exterior of the house, it was impossible for me to see into the crawl space. In fact, logs, timbers, scorched rubber tires and partially burned newspaper crammed the space under the house. This attempt at arson was one for the books and not surprisingly, the homeowner and now claimant, was using the SODDIT (some other dude did it) defence which would have been somewhat credible; had the client not been way over his head in personal debt.

Exercising due diligence, I canvassed neighbours living around the large remote lake and learned that most people only lived on the lake during the summer months, and used their lakeside homes as cottages and not permanent residences. However, there was one resident living on the other side of the lake that knew the claimant and had heard in the small village ten miles down the road, that the claimant regularly talked about the lack of fire department response time, should there ever be a fire. The homeowner went on to lament that he could not afford to live on the lake anymore, and his insurance rates were exorbitant as a result of the distance of a fire protection station. These two discussions, taken together in context with the fact that he was financially unable to pay his bills and lived in the remote area, was sufficient motive to suspect arson on the part of the owner.

Knowing that arson in itself does not preclude an insurance claim from being paid, as the burden on the Crown to prove arson requires motive, opportunity and a physical connection to the scene. Although two of the three requirements were met to charge the homeowner, there was nothing to connect the owner to the fire scene. As the smoke damage to the crawl space and floor of the house was considered sufficient to open a claim, the owner was compensated for hiring a smoke restoration company and paid for someone to clean the debris out of the crawl space.

CHAPTER 39

Fire Scene Investigation #8
The Hot Wire

In early 1999, while extremely active in our business, a former provincial court Judge, a steady source of business for our company, invited me for lunch and during the repast, invited me to open a storefront investigations office in Honolulu, Hawaii. The former judge explained that he enjoyed golfing and thought that a store front investigations/law office would be a means to assist vacationing Canadians with bodily injury claims, while allowing us to enjoy the luxury of golfing on the Island of Oahu.

In my memoir *Buckshot & Johnnycakes*, I relate the story of going to Honolulu at the end of January 1999; writing the Hawaiian Private Detectives Examination, opening a storefront office and encountering roadblocks with the IRS and CRA. Roadblocks that miffed the former judge who decided that he was not going to pay double income tax for a few golfing trips per month. Reluctantly the grandiose plan was abandoned.

In retrospect, it proved to be a wise decision as, on December 16th 1999, I suffered an aortic stenosis requiring open-heart surgery to replace my aortic valve at the Royal Jubilee Hospital on December 31st, 1999. I was the last open-heart surgery of the century in Victoria, B.C. and my wife fondly calls me the *Millennium Man*. It was a devastating blow to our company and put our business on hold for approximately six months. However, concerned about losing clients and being forgotten about in the industry, we made it clear to fire departments that our company was physically able to stand security watches on fire scenes as the income would help keep the business afloat.

In early March, only three months into recovery, I received a late night phone call from the fire dispatcher of a municipal call centre in a large community requesting my presence at a single family dwelling fire scene on Walfred Mountain, west of Langford, B.C.

Arriving at the scene at approximately 3:00 a.m. dressed in full security uniform, I signed onto the fire scene and the fire chief, a personal acquaintance, advised me that the site was a crime scene and that they would be back in the morning with a Fire Causation team of investigators whom I also knew personally. As they departed, I made a full security round outside the nearly destroyed residence and then climbed into my security vehicle, waiting for the sun to come up over the mountain.

Early morning on the mountain is beautiful and while vigilantly watching for intruders, I noticed several large deer munching twigs and foliage not far from the truck window. It was delightful to see and, while I was enjoying nature and grateful for being alive, the fire investigative team arrived on site. Meeting the team at the taped off entrance to the property and signing in the crew of four investigators, the fire chief commenced a causation investigation.

It was interesting to see how my colleagues carried out the onerous and time consuming task of investigating a major fire scene and, as I was timidly walking around the nearly burned out residence a, 2700 hundred square foot three level home hidden from view of the road and neighbours and, looking down into the basement; the only area of the structure that was still intact, I noticed a melted and twisted collection of electrical transfer boxes stacked in a six foot wide by five foot deep pile. There were at least 35, ten inch metal electrical junction boxes and numerous bare electrical copper wires lying all over the basement floor. In the far north corner of the basement, west of the main roadway was a partially burned waterbed frame filled with melted plastic planting pots.

Watching the fire investigators working with shovels in the basement, I leaned over and said to the chief: "There seems to be a partial skeleton lying outside the wooden bed frame, do you want me to call the police?"

The chief, who was making his way to the waterbed filled with dirt, plant pots and wilted marijuana leaves loudly intoned: "Stop, everyone be quiet! Do you hear that clicking sound?"

Everyone including me, stopped what they were doing and headed over towards the chief. Of course, I was quite enthralled by the sudden silence and began walking around the perimeter of the basement foundation, with the intention of going down the ladder to see what the chief was talking about. However, before I could move the chief pointed towards my position and said:

"I think that clicking noise is his new mechanical heart valve!"

The tension immediately lifted and everyone had a good laugh at my expense. Not to be daunted, I navigated over to the ladder and gingerly made my way down to the basement floor, stepping through the debris before stopping near the pile of bones lying on the concrete floor. While scrutinizing chalky, partially burned bones, one of the fire investigators leaned down and picked up what appeared to be a vertebra and, lifting the bone to his mouth, licked the bone and said: "Nope, not human." Of course, several of the other investigators snorted in disgust as the chief looked at me and nodded assent.

Looking around at the bemused faces visibly shocked that the senior investigator had licked the burned bone, I responded: "Animal bones do not have the same density as human bones and if the tongue does not stick to the bone it is usually human: a quick way to save having to send the bones to a forensic lab."

It was an amusing interlude and we all knew that the bones had to be sent to the lab; although we felt sorry for the dog that had died in the basement while the tenant was not at home: a fact that became evident later during neighbourhood enquiries. We also knew that the fire had been caused by arson and the chief asked me to accompany him on a perimeter search.

Going back up the ladder accompanied by the Fire Chief, we commenced a perimeter search and while walking around the front side of the house, through a large patch of juniper bushes, the fire chief tripped and fell to his knees. Moving to his side, we both noticed a large electrical coax cable partially buried under the ground. When the chief pulled on the electrical cable we could see that the wire was directly in line with the basement electrical junction boxes. Turning the other way, he pulled up on the electrical cable and moving and pulling the cable at the same time we traversed the garden bed towards the roadway and through the bushes. Arriving at the edge of the property we noticed the cable running up the side of a wooden hydro pole. The cable was held in place by large metal staples. The wire cable terminated at a large junction box attached at the top of the pole. It was time to phone the police.

It was amazing that the tenant, a 22-year-old male, who the police had been looking for since the fire was discovered; had managed to run the electrical cable out from under the house, bury the coax cable in the yard and run it up the telephone pole. Concerned now that there might be other skeletal bones in the basement; a more thorough search was made.

Helping the chief with the fire investigation, we found a rectangular piece of carpeting lying on the basement floor directly beneath where the back door of the house had been before the upper structure went up in flames. The carpet sample proved to be soaked in an accelerant, which later tested as being lighter fluid.

The determination was that someone had opened the back door, poured a large amount of lighter fluid on the carpet inside the doorway, ignited the carpet and left the scene, probably not knowing that the dog was downstairs in the basement.

A search of the land titles registry established that the owner of the stately and expensive house also owned three other rental properties, lived in a different city and that all three of those homes had been destroyed by fire. The case was never concluded and the insurance claim was paid, while the tenant was charged with operating a grow-op.

Having spent nearly 12 hours onsite, the chief turned the crime scene over to my security company and, shortly after the fire team investigators departed, an RCMP Criminal Investigation Section constable arrived on scene and advised that he was waiting for the forensic team to arrive.

Not much later, one of my security guards took over the site as our company was required to remain on security watch until the scene was released to the insurance company. An interesting postlude to this case is that several years later the insurance industry, through enacting legislation was successful in getting legislation in place that allowed the justice system to seize property from negligent landlords under the *Proceeds of Crime Act*. The new legislation virtually made absentee landlords fully responsible for criminal activity perpetrated by tenants renting or leasing their property.

CHAPTER 40

Taking down the Shingle

On December 31st, 2016, we closed our investigations company and retired to the highways in our recreational vehicle; although we still maintain our investigators licences to remind us of the 26 incredible years that we were remunerated for our exciting work and amusingly entertained in the process. We are proud to have been a professional resource in our country and the United States. It was a grand idea to" hit the road" and we travelled all over North America in our RV.

Five years before retiring from our investigations business, I began working as a Command Service officer with BC Yukon Command of the Royal Canada Legion as a Pension Disability officer working with Veterans Affairs Canada. My office was in the Joint Personnel Support Unit (JPSU) at Canadian Forces Base Esquimalt where I worked in that job until retiring from that rewarding vocation in 2014, although I continue working as a volunteer veterans' advocate to this day.

Living in the community of Lake Cowichan during that period of time, I wrote a true-life memoir: *Buckshot & Johnnycakes* about my best friend Brian Bomford (Buckshot) whom I met at the age of 11 in the Cowichan Valley. Our amazing friendship, filled with hilarious adventures, lasted fifty-six years until his death on May 2nd, 2013. He was far too young to leave this earth and we miss him every day.

After writing *Guilty Knowledge,* I am contemplating writing a third book chronicling my adventures in the Royal Canadian Navy and Canadian Forces.

ABOUT THE AUTHOR

Allan W. Waddy

The author, professionally known as "Ace", joined the Royal Canadian Navy at the age of eighteen and traveled around the globe before retiring as a Naval Officer in 1988. Upon retiring from the military, Allan worked as a Corrections Officer, Zone Manager Provincial Emergency Program (Police Services Branch) as a peace officer, an Executive Assistant and Ministerial Assistant for two Provincial Cabinet Ministers. After leaving government in 1990, Allan started **Ace Investigations & Security** until closing that business on December 31, 2016. Currently, Allan works as an In-House investigator for a Nanaimo law firm. Allan has been a passionate Veterans advocate for over thirty-five years and continues to assist Military and RCMP members with veteran benefits.